Mental Health Nursing
and
Social Control

Mental Health Nursing and Social Control

Peter Morrall PhD, MSc, BA (Hons), PGCE, RGN, RMN, RNMH

School of Healthcare Studies
University of Leeds

Whurr Publishers Ltd
London

© 1998 Whurr Publishers Ltd
First edition published 1998
by Whurr Publishers Limited
19b Compton Terrace, London N1 2UN, England

Reprinted 1999

British Library Cataloguing in Publication Data
A catalogue record for this book is available from the
British Library.

ISBN 1 86156 050 8

Printed and bound in the UK by Athenaeum Press Ltd,
Gateshead, Tyne & Wear

Contents

For my father
Dr. Alan Morrall
requiescat in pace

Introduction

'The world is all grown strange. Elf and Dwarf in company walk in our daily
fields; and folk speak with the Lady of the Wood and yet live; and the Sword
comes back to war that was broken in the long ages ere the fathers of our
fathers rode into the Mark! How shall a man judge what to do in such times?'
(Éomer in The Lord of the Rings, J R R Tolkein).

Mental health nursing has always been susceptible to modification
because of, for example, new treatments and changing demands by society (Peplau, 1994). However, the age has long past when a person qualified as a Registered Mental Nurse, and not only had 'employment for
life', but knew exactly what that job would entail. Today, there are no
reliable assurances about the direction of psychiatric nursing.

As one of the tribe of 'conference groupies', I find myself pursuing
the 'stars' of the mental health scene at national and international
venues, in the company of equally bewildered and ontologically insecure colleagues, attempting to discover what should be the way forward. In the Foucaudian tradition of 'knowledge archaeology', the
members of this tribe engage in a pathetic and unrealisable 'dig' for the
truth. As we end one millennium and begin another, veracity has
become elusive.

Not only is there little cohesion among politicians and leaders of the
mental health disciplines, but frequently I observe incongruity and contradiction in my own views. Sometimes within the same conversation I
deliver a diatribe on the need to 'empower' such socially marginalised
groups as the mentally disordered, then, lo and behold, I am fervently
voicing concern about social order and the need to take seriously the
threat of violence from (some of) those people who are perceived as
'mad'.

But incoherent thinking is only to be expected. The world is in a
state of unprecedented flux. Staunchly socialist countries have become
democracies, political parties transform their ideologies to win elec-
tions, communications systems alter dramatically our sense of space

and time, science spawns what otherwise would have been left in the realm of 'Frankenstein' mythology, there may have been life on Mars after all, and respected professors of nursing argue for the exclusive use of Random Controlled Trials as a research methodology. However, what politicians, academics and leaders of such disciplines as mental health nursing advocate today, may not be the same as that which is promoted tomorrow.

The mental health industry itself is in chaos: 'Services for the mentally ill are in turmoil in many parts of Britain ... with Government plans setting out how mental patients ought to be cared for ... being widely ignored' (Fletcher, 1995).

Furthermore, mental health nursing is drowning under a deluge of policy initiatives, legislation and recommendations from reports and inquiries. In the past few decades, the mental health industry has been required to: accommodate the independent sector; disentangle purchasers from providers, and health care from social care; introduce care plans for patients discharged from hospital; offer non-custodial care and treatment to mentally disordered offenders; reduce morbidity and suicide rates among the mentally ill; give priority to people placed on supervision registers; implement a new mental health act; assess the risk of violence and homicide; replace care in the community with a 'spectrum' or 'continuum' of care; prepare for the possibility of an overarching planning and commissioning body; respond to the implications of the Patient's Charter; empower users and carers; audit clinical practice; 'adopt a host of propositions from a series of reviews about the role and education of psychiatric nurses; and, in the face of sustained criticism concerning competency, provide the means for the mental health disciplines to "pull together"' (Sainsbury Centre, 1997).

Within this context of specious and precarious social arrangements, and unabated advice and directives, I attempt to deliver a 'rational' interrogative on psychiatric nursing. Moreover, in what could be regarded as yet another intractable paradox of the era we belong to, I acknowledge that despite the logical presentation of argument and empirical evidence, other interpretations of the events described here could be made: 'I am not ... setting out to "tell it like it is", but rather saying "look at it this way" ' (Rogers, 1991, p10).

The specific issue being addressed in this book is the status of mental health nursing and the role this discipline plays in society. The aim is to respond to the following questions: What is the professional status of mental health nursing? What is the function in society of mental health nursing?

To answer these questions, literature relating to the status of nursing in general, and mental health nursing in particular, is reviewed extensively. Using theory from the sociology of the professions, and the findings from my own research into mental health nurses working in the community, I suggest that to survive as a distinct occupational group, nursing must relieve itself of the unattainable goal of professionalisation, and seek an alternative future.

The specific theoretical device employed in addressing the aim of the book has its roots in the sociology of Max Weber, and in particular his notion of 'social closure': 'the action of social groups who maximise their own advantage by restricting access to rewards (usually economic opportunities) to their members thus closing access to outsiders' (Abercrombie et al., 1994, p384).

It is Eliot Freidson's revision and application of 'social closure' to the study of professions that provides the conceptual foundation to my analysis of mental health nursing. However, indulging to a limited extent in 'disciplined' eclecticism (Layder, 1994), I am indebted also to the insights derived from the work of Louis Althusser, Anthony Giddens, Andrew Scull and those intellectual revelations radiating from the body of knowledge that can loosely be described as 'clinical sociology'.

There are a number of concerns about definitions to deal with in this introduction. First, throughout the text I alternate between the use of the terms 'mental health nursing' and 'psychiatric nursing' as a matter of style. These two terms are used as synonyms. However, I am inclined towards the view that much of the work of 'mental' nursing remains directed towards dealing with 'illness' rather than promoting 'health'. Consequently, 'psychiatric nurse' remains more appropriate as a descriptive title.

What I mean by 'social control', a core theme of this book, also needs defining. Political, legal, religious, educational and medical institutions all play a part in maintaining the stability of a given society. Threats to society, or to those groups that have an interest in sustaining the social system (the wealthy and/or powerful), are curbed by these institutions. For example, criminals are gaoled, the immoral are excommunicated, disruptive pupils are expelled, new-age travellers are harassed, and the mad are incarcerated or supervised in the community. Social systems are liable to, and capable of, much adaptation to internal and external pressures. However, the fabric of a given society is intrinsically durable, and is only at risk of disintegration at times of momentous upheaval, such as civil war, famine, or economic collapse.

But categorical coercion by formal institutions is only part of the way in which society is controlled. What is much more pervasive and effective in preventing social disruption and decay is the commitment people have to shared values. Compliance is commanded through a myriad of informal networks:

'The powerful and often mystifying nature of the law, together with the visible presence of the police, can lead us to the conclusion that it is through these formal regulating institutions and agencies that social control is mainly exercised. But closer examination reveals that it is through the complex interplay of informal mechanisms that social control is primarily maintained. Indeed, the effectiveness and legitimacy of these formal institutions is ultimately dependent on the endorsement of these informal processes and the social attitudes which inform them' (Mathews, 1993, p28).

We are socialised into accepting the tenets and vagaries of a social system, therefore, through fear of condemnation by the 'agencies of social control', but, more importantly, by the positive and negative messages disseminated by friends, family, peers and the media (for example, television, cinema, newspapers and the Internet).

For Mathews, a corollary of this observation is that the reduction of crime can be achieved far more successfully through informal social control processes, such as 'neighbourhood watch' schemes. With reference to the control of deviant behaviour displayed by those people categorised as 'mad', the medical profession, assisted by the discipline of nursing, has formal powers to detain and, in certain circumstances, forcibly administer treatment. Scull (1993) observes that psychiatrists, as social control experts, are fundamental to the process of 'medicalising' certain behaviours, thereby diminishing the assumed threat to society. However, the intimate contact and rapport built-up between nurses and their clients can function as a veiled and far more influential social control measure, no matter how much their intentions are declared to be otherwise!

In chapter one, an overview is presented of the theories that have contributed to the understanding of the professions. This includes a review of functionalist, feminist, neo-Marxist, post-Fordist, managerialist, consumerist and post-modernist theories, as well as Freidson's medical-dominance thesis.

A critical analysis of the profession of medicine is provided in chapter two. Here, I argue that the profession of medicine, contrary to popular perception, remains powerful. Managerialism, consumerism, alternative health care, the rise of nursing and paramedical occupations, knowledge accessibility, and the processes of deprofessionalisation and proletarianisation, have not affected significantly the dominance of medicine. Moreover, I suggest that the power of medicine in society will be enhanced through developments in sophisticated technology, the 'drug revolution', biogenetics, and cyberspace.

In chapter three, there is an evaluation of the status of nursing, particularly in relation to the profession of medicine. I suggest that nursing is not, and cannot become, a profession because it has no legitimate ideology, its practice arena is diminishing, and health care assistants are replacing qualified nurses. Furthermore, I argue that many nurses are undermining the professionalisation of their discipline by accepting the role of surrogate 'junior doctor' and 'surgeon's assistant'.

The occupational position of mental health nursing in relation to both medicine and nursing in general, is explicated in chapter four. Specifically, the relationship between psychiatry and mental health nursing is explored, with particular emphasis on the social control function of both.

The next three chapters contain an account of the research I undertook into the professional status of community psychiatric nursing. This project is used as a case study of the social position of mental health nursing as a whole. First, the research project's rationale and design are detailed. In chapter six, the results are presented and discussed extensively. The implications of the results from the study are then explored in chapter seven. In particular, the results imply that when community psychiatric nurses gain clinical independence, and thereby appear to have achieved a key element of professionalism, it is only *de facto* (not *de jure*) autonomy.

If psychiatric nurses operating in the community do not possess authentic clinical freedom, then those who work within the various psychiatric institutions are constrained even further in their ability to become professionalised. Furthermore, the medical profession continues to dominate nursing, and the domination of mental health nursing by psychiatry results in the former being tied to the 'social control' function of the latter. Also discussed are the issues of a 'lack of rigour', underfunding, the 'moral panic' about madness and dangerousness, and the restructuring of mental health nursing to deal primarily with serious and enduring mental illness.

Finally, although I am cautious about making general assumptions, on the basis of the theoretical and empirical evidence submitted here, the argument is made for substituting professionalism with a strategy that necessitates the realignment of nursing with the medical profession. Psychiatric nurses would reassert their traditional allegiance with psychiatrists, and also accept an explicit social control function.

This is an expeditious and pragmatic tactic for psychiatric nursing. It would help to define a discrete role for psychiatric nurses, and thereby assist in the survival of the discipline. Furthermore, it would meet the demands of a society in the throes of an apparent 'moral panic' about the perceived dangerousness of the mentally ill living in the community, while at the same time helping to protect this group of vulnerable and marginalised people: 'Rarely a week goes by without another schizophrenic being turned away from a psychiatric unit, only to be found either dead in a ditch or guilty of a violent crime' (Launer, 1996).

However, I conclude that there may be another way forward for a section of psychiatric nursing. A band of nurses could become part of a radical force in psychiatry, assisting in the potent empowerment of the mentally disordered. Moreover, just as anti-psychiatry in the 1960s operated as a brake on the hegemonic, organic and overzealous 'control-orientated' tendencies of conventional psychiatry, this force could assuage the excesses of positivistic biomedicine in the next millennium.

Chapter 1
The Professions
in Society

An overview of the sociological theories that strove to comprehend the nature of the professions in the division of labour of contemporary capitalist societies is provided in this chapter. At the end of the 20th century, the nature of western societies is described in a number of ways by different social commentators. Bell (1973) uses the term 'post-industrial', Giddens (1990; 1991) and Tester (1993) 'late modernity', Lyotard (1985) 'post-modernity' and Jones (1995) 'cybersociety'. However, what is common to all these authors is the acceptance that western social systems are experiencing rapid change. This change is subsequently affecting the social, political, economic and cultural fabric of other societies throughout the world.

The professions are not immutable social institutions (Turner, 1995) and therefore have no inherent immunity from the influence of these changes. The conceptualisation of their role and function in society has had (or will have) to alter accordingly. Indeed, in the late 20th century, the professions can be detected to be going through a period of major transition. The well established professions of law and medicine may have to change their previously secure relationships with the state, the consumer, other occupations, and society in general (Dingwall and Lewis, 1983). Ultimately, in the case of medicine, this could result in a loss of control over health care resources (Armstrong, 1990).

Early 20th century explanations of what constitutes a profession were dominated by two related approaches, which were rooted in the sociology of Emile Durkheim (Johnson, 1972; Saks, 1983; Willis, 1990). Durkheim (1957) regarded the professions as an impartial and socially cohesive force. For Durkheim, they moderated individualism in society by reinforcing organic solidarity. That is, the depiction of society as an entity 'greater than the sum of its parts' is fortified by the professions' apparent devotion to the welfare of the community.

The first of the two post-Durkheimian approaches 'became concerned with definitional issues ... about what "traits" define a profession and how far along the process of professionalisation various occupations are' (Willis, 1990, p9).

Altruism, a specialised and exclusive body of knowledge, lengthy vocational training, monopoly over practice, and self-regulation were perceived to be the trade marks of high prestige occupations such as law and medicine (Carr-Saunders and Wilson, 1933; Goode, 1957; Greenwood, 1957; Gross, 1958).

The second approach is much more overtly functionalist. Here, the professions are regarded as helping directly to maintain the social order (Parsons, 1949, 1951; Barber, 1963). For example, Parsons (1949) argues that the profession of medicine reinforces social stability by, for example, controlling entry into the sick role. This benefits not only society as a whole, but also the individual in the sense that she or he receives expert assistance to become healthy again. Both of these perspectives 'rest on the tenet that professions possess some unique characteristics which set them apart from other occupations and play a positive and important role in the division of labour in society' (Saks, 1983, p2).

The trait and the functionalist approaches have been subjected to much criticism. The criticism is centred on the sterile nature of the teleological explanatory framework in which they are situated, and the stance of self-justification they adopt. For example, with reference to trait theory, Johnson (1972) states: ' "Trait" theory ... too easily falls into the error of accepting the professionals' own definition of themselves. There are many similarities between the "core elements" as perceived by sociologists and the preambles to and contents of professional codes' (p25).

Although the functionalist approach has the strength of being located in a general social theory (Morgan et al., 1985), both explanations are weakened by their inability to recognise and decipher other non-normative social processes and structures that fashion, and are fashioned by, the professions. For example, Johnson (1972) argued that these perspectives neglected to identify the power structures that are operated by the professions. He suggested that power could be exercised in different ways by different occupational groups. Members of a complete or 'collegiate' profession (e.g. medicine) exert power in a way that defines its membership, areas of work and who the users of its service will be. Members of a 'patronage' profession (e.g. accountancy) wield power in contractual arrangements that occur between themselves and the users of their services. Members of a 'mediated' profession (e.g. nursing) have less direct power as their services are provided via a third person or possibly the state.

Feminist critiques have also pointed to the weakness of the early sociological analysis (Gamarnikow, 1978; Hearn, 1982; Witz, 1990,

1992; Riska and Weger, 1993; Russell, 1995). These critiques have demonstrated that inequalities and oppression in the wider society are replicated by the professionals. With reference to medicine, they have revealed the centrality of gender divisions both within and between the various health occupations:

> 'Feminists have argued that in the process of upward mobility, the male-dominated professions gain control over and subordinate female-dominated occupations. This is most clearly demonstrated in medicine where the medical profession is male dominated and where in the process of achieving its dominant professional status, the female occupations of nursing, health visiting and midwifery were subordinated' (Abbott and Wallace, 1990, p3).

However, it is not only the structure of society on the basis of gender that has to be considered. Ethnic distinctions are also reproduced in the division of labour. For example, in the NHS (which is the biggest employer of ethnic minority groups in Britain: Ward, 1993) black employees are noticeably disadvantaged. Proportionally, they are much more likely to be employed in low status and low paid occupations than white people. They also hold lower status positions in both nursing and medicine, and enter the specialisms in these occupations, which have little prestige (e.g. psychiatry), much more frequently than their white counterparts (Johnstone, 1989).

The reasons for the inequalities in the NHS can be explained in part by reference to personal and institutional racism (Nettleton, 1995). However, the causes of these inequalities can be traced back to the history of imperialism and colonialism, and to the recruitment patterns of the British government in the 1950s (Williams, 1989).

McCulloch (1995) posits that it is impossible to detach the history of the medical profession in European countries from that of their colonial heritage. McCullock examines the part played by 'ethnopsychiatry' in preserving the white settler's opinion of the black African as a 'flawed' human being. Ethnopsychiatry was a term used by its practitioners and detractors to describe a medical and anthropological discipline that existed from the beginning of this century until the 1960s.

The British and French empires in Africa provided the conditions under which ethnopsychiatry could be founded. It lasted only as long as these conditions persisted. Ethnopsychiatric practice and research was embraced by Europeans faced by rising African nationalism. The pronouncements of the ethnopsychiatrists were used to justify the perception that the indigenous peoples failed as citizens, were unworthy of equal status with Europeans and were incapable of running their own countries.

The thrust of polemicist Ivan Illich's vehement critique of the professions is directed towards the process of industrialisation. Illich believes industrialisation has produced 'disabling' rather than 'helping' professions, and argues that: 'The Age of Professions will be remembered as the time when politics withered, when voters, guided by professors, entrusted to technocrats the power to legislate needs, renounced the authority to decide who needs what and suffered monopolistic oligarchies to determine the means by which these needs shall be met' (Illich et al., 1977, p12).

For Illich, the medical establishment has put both the health of individuals and society in jeopardy as a consequence of doctor-inflicted injuries and 'iatrogenic' dependency (Illich, 1977). Irving Zola (in Illich et al., 1977) argues that the profession of medicine has displaced the influence of religion and law in society. For Zola, medicine is now the pre-eminent instrument of social control. Through the doctrine of 'healthism', the medical profession has become the 'repository of truth', whereby the opinions of doctors hold great sway over the daily lives of the general population. Virtually all areas of our day-to-day activities, suggests Zola, have been infiltrated by medical representations of what is normal (health) and what is abnormal (ill health). That is, our whole existence has become 'medicalised'.

Illich offers a 'radical utopian' solution to the disempowering effect of the professions. He predicts an eventual nemesis for the professions: 'Professional cartels are now as brittle as the French clergy in the age of Voltaire; soon, the still inchoate post-professional ethos will reveal the iron cage of their nakedness ... But unbeknownst to them their credibility fades fast. A post-professional ethos takes shape in the spirit of those who begin to see the emperor's true physiognomy' (Illich, in Illich et al., 1977, p37).

Illich advocates the de-professionalisation of all professions, together with the de-industrialisation of the developed world's economic base. Industrial society would be replaced by a system of 'intermediate' technology. He argues also for the retention and protection of craftwork. Technological production would be based on the needs of the community, rather than on the over-stimulated 'wants' created by the monolithic and alienating industrial conglomerates – and the professionals.

The problem with the radical utopian approach is that, apart from spontaneous revolution, there is little elucidation on how industrial society is to go through such a transformation. Nor is there qualification of exactly what is meant by 'intermediate technology', or what mechanisms would be put in place, on the one hand, to prevent unacceptable growth and, on the other, to ensure against technological decline (Richman, 1987).

Moreover, since the 1970s (when Illich began his crusade for smaller scale and locally based economies), the economic agenda has altered spectacularly. Despite the existence of a number of experiments in 'intermediate technology' found in various parts of the world, supranational economic developments, aided by global communication networks, have produced a 'universal market'. Industrialisation and capitalism have expanded rather than contracted. Furthermore, the former socialist countries in Eastern Europe, with their proclaimed needs-led economies, are attempting to respond to the industrial exigencies of capitalism. Communist China, facilitated by the reclaimed Hong Kong, is unashamedly industrialising on a massive scale.

Marx (1969) perceived the role of the professionals in capitalist society as subsidiary, mainly because of their lack of direct involvement in the process of production. For example, Navarro (1979) sees the professionals aligned unambiguously with the capitalist class. They are, for Navarro, part of the exploitative elite in society. Professional groups contribute to the 'legitimisation of production under capitalist conditions by contributing to the management and surveillance of the working class ... The professionals exercise control on behalf of the capitalist class under the auspices of the state' (Turner, 1995, p130).

Scull (1979; 1983; 1984) refers to the specific role of psychiatry (a branch of the profession of medicine) as an agency of social control that serves the capitalist state by keeping 'the mad' (one section of the proletariat) under control. For Scull, psychiatry has been complicit in the implementation of a state-sponsored policy 'built on a foundation of sand' (1984, p1), which has resulted in the mentally ill (and other segregated groups) being decarcerated into the community.

The deinstitutionalisation of the mentally ill, argues Scull, is not the result of progressive developments in liberal-scientific psychiatry. Rather than the policy being driven by benevolence and the introduction of anti-psychotic drugs, it has been economically determined. Indeed, Scull argues that the reduction in the number of in-patients started in both the United States and the United Kingdom either before or during the 1950s, whereas anti-psychotic drugs were only beginning to be used in the middle of the 1950s. Scull's point is that in the postwar period, there was a fiscal crisis in the delivery of social policy whereby 'segregative modes of social control became, in relative terms, far more costly and difficult to justify' (Scull, 1984, p135).

Consequently, cheaper welfare options were sought, one of which was the programme of community care for the mentally ill. In part, Scull supports this position by suggesting that the former asylum inmates were not offered effective (and expensive) care in the community, but were neglected and ghettoised. Although Scull recognises that the pattern of decarceration in this country has been different to some degree from that in the United States, the rise in the number of the mentally ill who are homeless and live in bed and breakfast accommodation, can be viewed as examples of the ghettoisation and neglect of the mentally ill in the community (Murphy, 1991; Craig et al., 1995).

However, Scull's approach can be criticised in a number of ways. For example, Busfield argues that with respect to the United Kingdom, Scull's account is defective on the basis of timing: 'The fiscal crisis of the state to which he refers is a phenomenon of the early 1970s and later, and not of the 1950s' (Busfield, 1986, p329).

Busfield suggests that although Scull is correct to identify a 'mystification and distortion of a reality of neglect and lack of resources to those discharged from mental hospitals', he ignores the expansion of psychiatric services into primary health care. Referring specifically to the United Kingdom, and in direct contrast to Scull, Wing and Olsen (1979) offer an optimistic view on the implementation of care in the community. They claim that not only has care in the community been resourced through general practitioner services, but many other services have been developed, for example, local out-patient departments, day hospitals, rehabilitation workshops, community nursing and voluntary services.

Furthermore, far from viewing psychiatry as serving the capitalist class, some social theorists believe that the professionals have become proletarianised or de-professionalised (Haug, 1973; Oppenheimer, 1973; McKinlay and Stoeckle, 1988). A number of neo-Marxists who take this approach have described professionals, along with other middle class groups who earn their wage through selling their intellect, as 'mental labourers' (Wright, 1980; Derber, 1982). As such, professionals are in no more powerful a position within capitalist society than those who toil physically. This has been caused through a prolonged process of de-skilling as a result of the subordinate association that the professions have with state bureaucracies.

A synthesis of these two divergent notions of where the professions fit into the class structure is offered by another group of neo-Marxists (Carchedi, 1975; Gough, 1979). As Pilgrim and Rogers note, the professions are regarded by these theorists as occupying a contradictory relationship with the means of production in capitalist society: 'They are not capitalists but they serve the interests of the latter. They are not full members of the proletariat (as they do not produce goods and surplus value) but they are employees and so they share similar vulnerabilities and interests of the working class' (Pilgrim and Rogers, 1993, p84).

Interestingly, some theorists have argued that the achievement of a professional status is most likely for those occupational groups that have social and cultural affinity with the dominant groups in society (Johnson, 1977; Witz, 1992). That is, if the occupational group in question is male dominated and middle class, then it is in a better position to achieve and/or maintain a professional identity.

Post-structural accounts of the professions identify what Foucault (1967; 1973) describes as 'discursive practices' (i.e. particular technologies, procedures and linguistic styles) which act as mechanisms of social subjugation through a control over knowledge. Foucault gave the example of psychiatry regulating morality, rationality and the work ethic in bourgeois society. However, unlike the neo-Marxist analysis of the professions, which emphasises their structural relationship with the mode of production (i.e. whether or not they belonged to the proletariat or the bourgeoisie), the discursive practices of the professionals are not aligned ideologically with any one social class.

The successful, if tenuous, use of controlling techniques by one group of professionals – surgeons – is illustrated in a research study carried out by Fox (1992). He conducted an analysis of a health care setting (i.e. surgical wards and theatres) from which he attempted to demonstrate the relationship between power and knowledge. In a deconstruction of what Fox describes as 'the enterprise of surgery' (1993, p62), he comments on how the various disciplines attempted continually to register their respective discursive practices on each other, as well as on the patients. For example, Fox reflects on the hidden meaning of the 'practice' of asepsis:

> 'Asepsis acts not only as a bacteriological insurance, but also as a rhetorical marker of the process of surgical resection – as being something different to other assaults on the integrity of the body. For surgeons to possess a legitimacy for what they do (and hence a status other than that of a butcher or barber), these markers are clearly important, and this early analysis suggests a way of understanding how surgeons achieve and sustain their status and authority' (Fox, 1992, p128).

Hughes (1958), nearly 40 years ago, had already sown the conceptual seeds of dissension, which were to germinate into a debacle of the idealised definition of a 'profession'. However, it was the systematic theorising of Eliot Freidson (1970a; 1970b; 1988) which was to make the most significant impact on the trait and functionalist approaches. It was Freidson who was among the first to identify that the professions may primarily be serving themselves rather than their patients or society, and to indicate (together with Johnson, 1972) that the exercise of 'power' had to be taken into account:

> 'Freidson ... undercut the functionalist argument that professions were ordained by the "hidden hand" of society, exposing the power games which must be played for successful professionalisation ... He stressed that the medical profession, like any other, pursues its own ends in preserving its members' autonomy and privileges' (Richman, 1987, p110).

Freidson applied a neo-Weberian perspective and produced a coherent theoretical deconstruction of medicine, which he uses as a model for the analysis of other professions. His proposition is that a dominant profession stands in an entirely different structural relationship to the division of labour than does a subordinate one, and that it is having autonomy over one's actions (and influence over the work of others) that defines a 'genuine' profession.

Summary

The professions, like all social organisations, are liable to mutation as a consequence of major developments on a global basis. In this chapter, I have reviewed competing theories that attempt to uncover what the character of a profession is, what the motives of its practitioners are, and what role it plays in society. I have concluded, however, that 'power' is at the core of a critical understanding of the professions. Furthermore, I suggest that it is Freidson's thesis that still provides the most rectified exposé on how professional groups maintain their position of power.

Chapter 2
The Profession of
Medicine

In this chapter, the present position of medicine as a profession is analysed critically in order to establish the occupational status of nursing in general and mental health nursing in particular. Relying heavily on Freidson's seminal analysis of the profession of medicine, and contrary to what has become the orthodox view in sociology, I posit that the profession of medicine (including psychiatry) remains relatively powerful. The dominance of medicine has not been affected significantly by managerialism, consumerism, alternative health care, the rise of nursing and paramedical occupations, knowledge accessibility, and the processes of deprofessionalisation and proletarianisation. Moreover, I suggest that the power of the medical profession is escalating because of the substantial and abundant developments in technology, pharmacology, biogenetics and cyberspace.

Altruism

Freidson's approach was pivotal to the movement away from comprehending the division of labour in society solely on the basis of core traits and functions. What Freidson accomplished was a reformulation of the question about professions. He argued that the concentration on issues of definition had produced descriptive rather than analytical accounts of how professions operate: 'A great many words have been spoken in discussions of what a profession is, or rather, what the best definition of "profession" is. Unfortunately, discussion has been so fixed on the question of definition that not much analysis has been made of the significance and consequences of some of the elements common to most definitions' (Freidson, 1970b, p133).

Freidson directed attention towards the use of social closure and occupational control by some occupations to achieve professional status (Morgan et al., 1985; Nettleton, 1995). Medicine, for example, has gained high social prestige by restricting who can practise what it designates as 'medical' and 'surgical' procedures. Moreover, medical practitioners have expanded continuously into the physical, interpersonal, social and even spiritual aspects of the life of an individual.

For Freidson, the medical profession was motivated far more by self-interest than its proclaimed altruistic intentions, and the theoretical tenets of functionalism, would imply. Indeed, R Porter, (1996) has described the ambivalent attitudes of the public towards doctors. He is doubtful of a halcyon past when people respected and trusted doctors, arguing that there has been a great deal of scepticism about the efficacy of surgical and medical procedures throughout history.

An exploration of whether or not professional groups subjugate their own interests in favour of their patients, and society as a whole, has been carried out by Saks (1995). He examined how the medical profession responded to the growth and concomitant threat of acupuncture to biomedical hegemony in Britain. He concludes: 'The most striking feature of the analysis of the medical reception of acupuncture in this country over the past two centuries is the doubt shed on the extent to which the medical profession in general and its elite in particular has been characterised by altruism' (Saks, 1995, p260).

Knowledge

The assumption that medicine owes part of its success to specialist knowledge is challenged by Larson (1977). Larson argues that the medical profession linked up with biomedical science as a strategy aimed at ameliorating occupational and social advancement. As Armstrong has noted: 'In this new analysis, the success of a profession was not due to possessing the requisite "core traits" such as esoteric knowledge, a service ideal, and so on, but depended entirely on the degree of control the profession had managed to establish over the conduct of its own work' (Armstrong, 1990, p691).

That is, rather than biomedical science being an inherent and natural feature of medicine's epistemology, it used this form of knowledge as 'ideological ammunition for attaining the powerful position of professional status, as well as for maintaining it' (Morgan et al., 1985, p109).

Jamous and Peloille (1970) suggested that another strategy adopted by medicine to achieve occupational progress was to socially distance itself from the users of its service by mystifying the knowledge that it has. That is, the more medical practitioners are regarded as employing intuition, which cannot be codified, and the less the public has direct access to their specialist knowledge, the higher the social status of medicine. This is described by these authors as the 'indeterminacy/technicality (I/T) ratio'. However, there is a paradox here in that biomedical data (the medical profession's preferred knowledge base) are highly susceptible to codification. Furthermore, intuition is regarded as a characteristic of those occupational groups with a lower status than medicine. Therefore, medicine cannot rely on this strategy alone.

Autonomy

For Freidsonian theorists, the main method by which medicine and other professions attain high status is through the acquisition of discrete areas of work (Freidson, 1970a, 1988; Berlant, 1975; Larson, 1977; Tolliday, 1978). That is, the power of the medical profession depends on a large amount of autonomy over clinical work: 'The only true important and uniform criterion for distinguishing professions from other occupations is the fact of autonomy – a position of legitimate control over work' (Freidson, 1970a, p82).

This control with respect to medicine, argues Freidson, is legitimised through social and legal recognition of medical practitioners as experts who, as a group, are virtually unopposed in their ability to define health and illness:

> 'If we consider the profession of medicine today, it is clear that its major characteristic is pre-eminence. Such pre-eminence is not merely that of prestige, but also of expert authority. This is to say, medicine's knowledge about illness and its treatment is considered to be authoritative and definitive ... there are no representatives in direct competition with medicine who hold official policy-making positions related to health affairs' (Freidson, 1988, p5).

Not only has medicine gained control over its practice, but it also dominates what Freidson (1970b) describes as the 'paramedical professions' (for example, midwifery and nursing). Autonomy over its own work, and control over the content and limits of the work of related occupational groups, provides medicine with 'professional dominance' (Freidson, 1970b). A profession for Freidson, therefore, has autonomy from the subjugation of others, and has the autonomy to subjugate others.

Psychiatry

Baruch and Treacher (1978) argue that psychiatry, as a branch of medicine, has presided over the mental health industry in Britain since the 19th century. This dominance can be related to the rise of care of the mentally ill in asylums. It was the role of the psychiatrist as administrator, rather than that of skilled and effective practitioner, that provided the opportunity for a power base to be established in the asylum (Scull, 1979, 1993; Rogers and Pilgrim, 1996).

Psychiatrists enacted control over those who were considered to be harmful to society and, in particular, to Victorian mores and the Protestant work ethic. They operated as the 'moral guardians' of the conspicuously mentally disordered. However, Russell (1995) records that in France, where the asylum movement began, other groups of people came under the reign of medical administration. These included: single mothers; rebellious children; promiscuous women; the alcoholic; and the elderly. But, by the middle of the 19th century, the asylums had become focused on dealing with the mad (Scull, 1993).

The mad were separated from other corruptible and corrupting sections of the population, incarcerated in bureaucratic and isolated institutions. Here the specialism of 'mad-doctoring' was to flourish in a state-sponsored social control apparatus for the insane.

Although it has been suggested that the demise of the asylums as the locale for psychiatric care has resulted in the fragmentation of medical dominance (Samson, 1995), Bean and Mounser argue cogently that the structural position of psychiatry has become stronger in the 20th century:

> 'Psychiatrists have exchanged their traditional power-base in mental hospitals to expand into general hospitals alongside the physicians and the surgeons, as well as out into the community to encroach on the GPs' domain, presenting themselves as "experts" in the care of the mentally ill. They have expanded to present the world with an entourage – the multidisciplinary team, consisting of social workers, nurses, psychologists, behavioural therapists and occupational therapists. And these auxiliary staff now emulate the medical approach and, in doing so, reinforce the credibility of the power of psychiatry' (Bean and Mounser, 1993, p168).

It will be interesting to assess the effect on the structural omnipotence of psychiatry in the next century with the focus on 'primary' care for mental health services now being proposed (NHS Management Executive, 1996; Timmins, 1996). However, the influence of the medical profession as a whole will not necessarily be undermined whether the bulk of the service is delivered by psychiatry or in general practice.

Armstrong argues that the clinical autonomy of medicine has allowed the profession to exert control over the organisation of resources in health care:

> 'Medical power ... rested on a degree of autonomy in clinical work, which medicine had successfully claimed as its natural right ... In maintaining control over clinical work the medical profession established jurisdiction over the distribution of health care resources' (Armstrong, 1990).

If the definition of professional autonomy is to include the domination of other occupational groups, together with the control over health policy and resources, then autonomy for medicine is not absolute. As Freidson (1986) has admitted, professional autonomy is relative to the historical, structural, ideological and political parameters that encircle the negotiations that doctors (and other health care workers) undertake within both their organisational setting and society at large.

For example, Goldie (1977) carried out a study on the division of labour between mental health professionals working in psychiatric hospitals. He recognised that the professionalisation of any occupation cannot take place in a social vacuum. Goldie examined the role of ideology, alongside the way in which the division of labour is negotiated within the social structure of various institutional locations. For Goldie, the history of the psychiatric hospital and various internal and external 'institutional imperatives' (a term borrowed from Hearn, 1968), such as the resources and facilities available within the hospital and its catchment area, exert influences on the staff.

Goldie states that his research was concerned with: 'The complex task of reconciling certain "objective" features of the social structure of treatment settings found within mental hospitals, with the "subjective" views of these features as held by the staff who were interviewed ... Attention has to be paid to the way that actors themselves define their own situation, and how their actions, intentions and motivations form a dialectic with the institutions in which they participate' (Goldie, 1977, p142).

Negotiated Order Theory was employed by Goldie in his attempt to account for the interplay of professional practice, individual perceptions and motivations, and organisational control (Bucher and Strauss, 1961; Bucher and Stelling, 1969). Strauss et al. (1963) introduced the concepts of 'negotiated context' and 'structural context' to describe the relationship between individual action and formal rules, procedures and hierarchies within hospitals.

Although Goldie perceives mental hospitals as forums in which there are 'shifting balances of power' (1977, p145), he concludes that the psychiatrists sustain their dominance partly through their ideological monopolisation of the referral process, and partly through acquiescence of the other occupational groups: 'While many lay [i.e. non-medical] staff remain critical of the psychiatrists for their inadequate training and reliance on physical methods, they continually reaffirm their authority through a process of defining themselves out of certain areas of work and seeking to involve themselves in various marginal activities' (Goldie, 1977, pp158-9).

Therefore, the status quo in the professional hierarchy is maintained both by the overt use of power by psychiatrists and by the way in which the 'rival' professionals define their own roles.

Since Goldie's study, however, clinical psychologists have been perhaps the most active in attempting to redefine their role and relationship with psychiatry.

For example, Johnstone (1989), a senior NHS clinical psychologist, provides a vitriolic denunciation of the training and work of 'traditional' psychiatry. Psychology has produced clinical training programmes and treatment paradigms to contend with those of their medical counterparts. However, Rogers and Pilgrim (1996) observe that British clinical psychology is at present in a precarious position, with the suggestion that the discipline may be in decline. Specifically, they point to legislation (i.e. the 1990 NHS and Community Care Act), the implementation of which has undermined previous advances in the status of their discipline: 'Their role can be eroded by others and their employment is no longer guaranteed. The latter is a result of "treatment packages" being offered in modalities which potentially could be produced cheaper by other occupational groups (community mental health nurses or counsellors)' (Rogers and Pilgrim, 1996, p106).

De-professionalisation

The proletarianisation thesis (Oppenheimer, 1973; McKinlay and Stoeckle, 1988) projects the view that professional work is becoming increasingly subjected to management control at the instigation of the state. Supporters of this approach believe the fate of all professions to be downward social mobility. Haug (1988) argues that de-professionalisation will occur as a consequence of the rise in consumer scepticism about the efficacy of 'expert' services. Both of these critiques imply that bureaucratic processes will lead to the demise of professional autonomy and dominance. An example of the state-sponsored bureaucratic processes that can impinge on medical authority is that of the complaints procedures against doctors:

> 'Doctors' traditional stranglehold on NHS complaints is being threatened by [former] Health Secretary Virginia Bottomley ... Mrs Bottomley has said: "We believe the time has come to look, to uproot, to re-examine our mechanisms for dealing with complaints" ' (Bevins, 1993).

In Britain, the 1995 Medical (Professional Performance) Act has enshrined in legislation the onslaught by the state on the profession of medicine. This act means that doctors can now be sanctioned (to the point of being struck off the medical register) for simply not being good at their job, rather than, as in the past, having injured, sexually assaulted, or killed one or more of their patients (Collee, 1995).

However, as Elston (1991) and Nettleton (1995) have commented, the proletarianisation and bureaucratisation theories have emerged from the United States and their application to the British health care system has not been evaluated. In the past 20 years the I/T ratio has altered. There has been an explosion in information and access to information. Clinical knowledge has become more codified and less indeterminate. As Nettleton (1995) records, computerised expert systems (used, for example, in the diagnosis of illness) allow members of non-professional groups, and those groups striving to professionalise, entry into bodies of knowledge that were formerly esoteric.

Alternative Medicine

The perceived existence of a more active and knowledgeable service-user may also threaten to narrow the social distance between the patient and the medical practitioner (Hugman, 1991; Morrall, 1995c). This active service-user could also be seen to be challenging medical hegemony by consuming alternative health care provision (now widely available) such as acupuncture, homeopathy, osteopathy and chiropractice.

However, as Joseph (1994) recognises, there are signs that 'alternative' health care is formulating a set of beliefs and practices that will survey the boundaries of medicine, and serve to exclude 'unqualified' interlopers. Doctors are gradually substantiating their influence over alternative medicine by directing patients to these treatments, employing their practitioners within the formal health services, or by delivering the service themselves. This trend can be observed in the case of acupuncture (Saks, 1995), and now it is the turn of aromatherapy to be enveloped by medicine: 'Aromatherapy, once regarded as the preserve of cranks and "new-agers", has finally arrived in the mainstream and is becoming available on the NHS. The Royal Liverpool University Hospital is the first to provide aromatherapy as part of a range of alternative treatments' (Fowler, 1996).

In the United Kingdom, a medical practitioner (Craig Brown) has even been appointed as the president of the National Federation of Spiritual Healers (Illman, 1996). The effect of encompassing 'cranky' treatments within the NHS is to legitimise and control alternative provision within the boundaries of conventional medicine.

Management

From the 1980s onwards, in Britain, the structural and bureaucratic limitations on the clinical autonomy of the medical profession would include the restructuring of the health service and the rise of 'new managerialism'. New managerialism replaced what Harrison et al (1990) describe as the 'diplomacy model' which had existed since the 1960s.

Managers under the latter system were not leaders or agents of change. Their primary role was to help the professionals in their clinical work by solving organisational problems as they occurred. In contrast, the new managers are expected to be much more proactive, innovative, and consumer-oriented. This modernisation of the management style has been integral to the British Conservative government's overhaul of the NHS, aimed at a cost-effective, efficient, slimmer and leaner health care service (Jones, 1994). In part, it has involved the comprehensive auditing of clinical work, which, it can be argued, erodes further the autonomy of the professionals. In England alone, by the end of the century, more than £800 million will have been spent on encouraging health care practitioners to accept the auditing of their clinical work (Moore, 1997).

Such disciplines as nursing, occupational therapy, physiotherapy, psychology and speech therapy would seem to be on course to embrace the doctrine and procedures of 'audit' (Kogan et al., 1995). However, the profession of medicine has been much more aware of the peril to its freedom and has, accordingly, executed a programme of non-compliance: 'In principle, consultants and GPs have been required to review their performance and improve standards ... In practice, many doctors still resist, avoid and blankly refuse to undertake clinical audit or to act on its results' (Moore, 1997).

Such 'hostile' doctors are put under political pressure from both the Tory and Labour parties, health consumer groups and prominent academics such as Professor of Health Economics, Alan Maynard, who has lambasted the present situation as 'a shambles' (Moore, 1997). However, notwithstanding this onslaught of criticism, the auditing of medical practice that does take place remains under the command of the profession itself.

Paramedical Disciplines

The relationship between medicine and the paramedical disciplines, which Freidson perceives as one characterised by the domination of the former over the latter, is explored by a number of authors. For example, Stein (1967) discusses how nurses are involved in a 'game' with doctors. The nurses play this game by offering advice in subtle ways (for example, through indicating non-verbally what policies, treatments, etc. they agree with) to the medical staff, while appearing to be passive:

'The cardinal rule in the game is that open disagreement between the players must be avoided at all costs. Thus, the nurse can communicate her recommendations without appearing to be making a recommendation statement. The physician, in requesting a recommendation from a nurse, must do so without appearing to be asking for it' (Stein 1967, p110).

Wright (1985) also describes the relationship between doctors and nurses as a 'game'. There is, suggests Wright, an elaborate and ritualistic facade erected between the two. The nurse tries to manipulate the doctor's decisions without weakening 'his' authority or status. Overt disagreement is avoided at all costs.

Sam Porter, reporting on his observations of interactions between nurses and doctors working in an intensive care unit and a general medical ward, suggests that the power gap between the two disciplines may be closing; nursing subordination to medicine is more complex than previous studies indicate. However, he concludes: 'While nurses are becoming increasingly open in their contribution to decisions about care, doctors still possess considerable advantages over them, such as the comprehensiveness of their formal education and their legal status' (Porter, 1991, p728).

Tattersall (1992), in a study of triage in an accident and emergency department, noted that although this method of organising patients was instigated by nurses (and had the potential effect of enhancing the occupational status of the nurses in relation to that of the physicians), it was usurped by the medical staff. That is, the doctors recognised the effectiveness of triage, and thereby legitimised its use, only when they made decisions with regard to its implementation.

Hughes conducted a study of doctor-nurse interaction in an accident and emergency department. He criticises the professional-dominance thesis for presuming too much power to be in the hands of the medical profession:

> 'Many sociologists, possibly taking their cue from Freidson's ... seminal writings on the position of the "paramedical" professions have chosen to view the [nurse-doctor] relationship in terms of a fairly unproblematic subordination of nursing staff to physician control. Among other things they note that the medical profession exercises considerable control over the knowledge base of the nursing profession; that typically nurses assist in, rather than initiate the focal tasks of diagnosis and treatment; and that much nursing work tends to be performed at the request of, or under the supervision of the doctor' (Hughes, 1988, p1).

Although not wanting to debunk the professional-dominance thesis *per se*, Hughes believes that it needs one important qualification. He argues that it is 'over-deterministic', and its proponents have 'underplayed the situated nature of medical control and of nurse deference' (Hughes, 1988, p16).

As Hughes' adjustment to the professional-dominance thesis indicates, there is a clear need to examine the divergent situations among the health care professionals. For example, psychiatric nurses working in the community, as Carr et al. (1980) have pointed out, cannot be viewed as having the same relationship with psychiatrists as those nurses who work within the hospital environment. There are, for example, major differences in levels of medical (and managerial) surveillance and supervision of ostensibly subordinate occupational groups.

The effect of these situational factors in the health care field can be to reduce the professional dominance of one occupational group (e.g. the medical staff), while increasing the clinical autonomy of another (e.g. nurses). That is, if medicine loses its dominance over nursing (and other health care groups) it is axiomatic that the former will experience some degree of de-professionalisation, whereas the latter will move further towards professionalisation.

Post-Fordism

Another possible outcome may be a realignment of occupational loyalties as a consequence of the NHS reforms, and the post-Fordist division of labour (Harrison and Pollitt, 1994; Walby et al., 1994). Post-Fordist economic production is characterised by consumer-led and fragmented market requirements, and demands that its workers (including professionals) are flexible over working practices (Burrows and Loader, 1994). In this scenario, it is probable that professional autonomy will diminish (Nettleton, 1995).

In a post-Fordist mode of production, it is possible, however, that there will be a transformation in the relationships between the various occupational groups. For example, this new form of economic production may encourage nurses, who, for Dixon (1992), are 'organisationally adrift', to relocate their allegiance from their own managers to doctor-dominated NHS Clinical Directorates (Walby et al., 1994). That is, nursing may be far more vulnerable to the processes of 're-skilling', insecure employment and loss of professional autonomy, than medicine. Therefore, domination of medicine over other occupational groups (e.g. nursing) may be re-established.

Moreover, there is growing evidence that although medicine's direct control over organisational resources has been lost, it still procures a considerable amount of freedom from the new managers with regard to resource prioritising and clinical work at a local level (Haywood, 1987; Clegg, 1989; Hunter, 1991).

Baggott (1994), for example, states: 'It is clear that general managers made only limited progress in setting clinical targets ... Managers were largely unable to exert control over the resources for which they were held accountable because the demand for patient services was determined by clinicians' (p134).

Baggott (1994) argues that most managers have capitulated or resigned when confronted by senior doctors. One report by Professor Liam Donaldson (director of public health and regional general manager of the Northern and Yorkshire Regional Health Authority) has suggested that managers can do little about the 'one in 20' consultants who may be dishonest, abusive, guilty of sexually harassing patients, or incompetent (Mihill, 1994). The report concludes that most of these problems are ignored by managers, or the practitioner involved is encouraged to retire. Moreover, managers perceive themselves to be vulnerable to public and political scrutiny, and potential unemployment (Timmins, 1995).

The medical establishment has the flexibility to adapt to competing treatments, and also has the capacity to deal with political intimidation. For example, the British Medical Association has presented the case for doctors to be involved in policy making and managing the NHS (Brindle, 1995a; R. Porter, 1996). Furthermore, the editor of the British Medical Journal has drawn attention to the class and status similarities between doctors and managers, which suggests the two groups are more likely to be social, cultural, and political allies than they are foes:

> 'The senior members of both professions are very alike in their lifestyles, tending to vote Conservative, wear suits and ties, enjoy sport and middle-brow culture, take foreign holidays, send their children to private schools, and drink too much. Doctors and managers who row in the local newspapers may well belong to the same Masonic lodge' (Smith in Brindle, 1995a).

If the power of medicine were to be challenged seriously by the new managers or the government, then radical defensive strategies might be adopted. For example, the BMA has warned of 'militant resistance' if a government-instigated policy of paying doctors local rates is executed (Brindle, 1995b). This could also involve working only the hours formally contracted to the health service. Some medical practitioners have even proposed leaving the health service altogether:

> 'Senior doctors are threatening to resign from National Health Service employment and establish themselves as independent contractors to escape management diktat ... Consultants believe they would have more freedom to determine treatment according to patients' needs if they were free of managers' budget constraints' (Brindle and Mihill, 1994).

Cyber-power

Where do these influences leave the professional-dominance theses and the professional status of medicine? In the second edition of Freidson's 'Profession of Medicine' (1988), the content is essentially the same as the first edition, except that he includes an 'Afterword'. It is in this afterword and in a later text where he re-examines the role of the professions in society (Freidson, 1994) that Freidson addresses a number of the criticisms of his analysis of medicine. For example, he recognises the development of consumer movements, and the 'active' and knowledgeable service-user. However, he questions the effect these developments have had on the power of the professional:

'These movements have created a number of important changes in the administrative and interpersonal context within which interaction between doctor and patient takes place. However, while the traditional arrangement in which the physician is active or guiding and the patient passive or cooperative has been tempered somewhat, there is little evidence that it has changed so markedly as to have become routinely egalitarian, involving truly mutual participation' (1988, p388).

The growth of new contractual systems, observes Freidson, are, in essence, aimed at cutting costs, and may have had a detrimental effect on the patient's ability to be active in her or his relationship with the medical practitioner. In Britain, these systems would include the Conservative government's legislation which created NHS Trusts, the opportunity for general practitioners to become budget-holders, and a 'mixed economy' for welfare (DoH, 1989a; 1989b).

Freidson goes as far as to suggest that the collective gains from, for example, the consumer movements, may not compensate for the loss of influence individuals have experienced through these contractual arrangements.

However, the explosion of information is entering a dramatic, new phase (Freedland, 1994). Computer-based technology is now operating in a realm that has been described by William Gibson, in his 1994 novel 'Neuromancer', as 'cyberspace'. That is, through the Internet, consumers can gain access to immense and immediate banks of knowledge on a worldwide scale, the potential of which only the most Luddite-minded would want to ignore.

But in reality, this knowledge is not available to all. There is a 'cyber-underclass' – i.e. the significant proportion of the population that does not have the opportunity to gain the necessary skills to use contemporary technology, or cannot afford to buy the necessary equipment. Moreover, these information systems will be susceptible to expropriation by both established and new breeds of experts who have (or will have) the techniques and resources to analyse and synthesise data on this scale (Porter, 1994).

Given the imperialistic and market-oriented tendencies associated with medicine in the past (e.g. in relation to accommodating 'alternative' medicine as 'complementary' medicine), and its success in promoting a techno-scientific base in modern health care, future occupation strategies are likely to include expeditions into, and colonisation of, cyberspace.

The link between computer technology and the delivery of medical treatment is well developed, and has recently received a major boost. Leading computer and biotechnology industrialists have begun collaborative exercises using computers and biotechnology to produce drugs: 'Two of the computer industry's most successful entrepreneurs have joined forces with a leading biotechnology company. Bill Gates and

Paul Allen, cofounders of Microsoft, last week invested $10 million in Darwin Molecular, a company that hopes to use a better understanding of human genetics to design drugs' (Coghlan, 1994, p4).

Revolutionary Science

The profession of medicine is a dynamic and phagocytic enterprise. What count as legitimate areas of work for medical practitioners are changing and expanding constantly. The knowledge base of the medical profession alters according to trends and developments in what could be included broadly under the rubric of 'science and technology'. Medical practice is influenced also by consumer demands (e.g. for cosmetic surgery; hormone replacement therapy) and political pressures and constraints (e.g. fiscal control over the National Health Service).

Moreover, it is fallacious to portray the profession of medicine as being underpinned by a unitary and homogeneous 'medical model'. Seedhouse argues that it is naive, and part of a mythology propagated by sociologists, to argue that medicine is governed by science and technology. For example, the profession is divided into distinct specialisms. This results in very different forms of knowledge and treatments between the various medical factions. Even within the specialisms there are wide disparities:

> 'Although the 50-year-old psychiatrist, who is a strong advocate of psychotherapy, may have learnt his medicine at the same medical school at the same time as the 50-year-old Professor of Pharmacology and Therapeutics, to say that they both espouse precisely the same "medical model" must be demonstrably wrong. The two doctors practise their medicine in different ways, and apparently in accord with quite different tenets. One uses drugs only as last resort, the other sees drug therapy as central to the medical endeavour' (Seedhouse, 1991, p66).

However, medicine is in an expedient and reflexive relationship with the revolutionary advances taking place in theoretical physics and mathematics (e.g. chaos, catastrophic, superstring and 'complex' theories), technology, molecular and cell biology, evolutionary (neo-Darwinian) psychology, and pharmacology. That is, the profession is embracing an 'epidemic of techno-scientific discovery' (Nuland, 1996).

This scientific renaissance encompasses an immense and accelerating list of discoveries – for example: computed tomographical scanning; magnetic resonance imaging; computerised virtual reality imaging; positron emission tomography; arthroscope and laproscope surgery; microscopic surgery; remote surgery; in vitro fertilisation; gamete intrafallopian transfer; heart transplants from genetically altered pigs to humans; cornea, liver, pancreas, kidney and heart-lung transplants; artery and vein allographs; percutaneous transcatheter embolisation; novel anti-psychotic, anti-depressant, anti-dementia and anti-cancer drug designs; genome mapping, screening and diagnosis; electric stimulation of retinal nerve to cure some forms of blindness; lithotripter renal treatment; trans-cranial magnetic therapy for depression; neural grafting; and the cloning of human cells to help understand the ageing process, and replace damaged tissue.

But the potency of the profession of medicine rests in the continuation of a strategic dualism. First, as Clare (1976) has pointed out, medicine is eclectic. That is, its practitioners indulge in a huge variety of approaches, from cognitive-behavioural therapy to leucotomy, caesarean section to mastectomy, and hypnotherapy to electroplexy. Second, the application of the new techno-scientific knowledge to the field of health care expands and reinforces medical authority, or at least channels attention away from its limitations and failures. For example, highlighting the techno-scientific base of medicine tends to camouflage the social factors behind many of its apparent successes. As McKeown (1979) has argued, medicine was not fundamentally responsible for the decline in mortality rates caused by infectious diseases in the 19th century. For McKeown, improvements in diet, food hygiene, sanitation and housing (as a consequence of economic reforms) were far more influential than medical interventions.

Weatherall (1995) observes that medicine has still not conquered heart attacks, strokes, AIDS or the common cold. Despite improvements in treatment, the number of diabetics and asthmatics continues to grow, antibiotics are no longer as effective as they once were, malaria and cholera are endemic in parts of the world, and new diseases such as that caused by the Eboli virus still occur. Abraham (1995) suggests that the testing and control of pharmaceutical products continues to be far from satisfactory, exposing the public to further 'Thalidomide' incidents. Psychiatric theory that purports to grasp the complexities behind schizophrenia is deconstructed as 'scientific delusion' by Boyle (1993).

However, these deficiencies in the practice of medicine are counterbalanced by the well publicised promise of future accomplishments offered by the new techno-scientific knowledge. For example, Patel, writing in *The Times Higher Education Supplement*, discusses the stubborn refusal of tuberculosis to be eradicated in certain parts of the world, and its re-emergence in the West. The style of her article is positively evangelical about the propensity of medicine, using modern science, to tackle a disease that still causes more than three million deaths annually:

'The prospect of more powerful vaccines for the killer disease tuberculosis being available in the near future looks more promising thanks to an important advance in genetic engineering by scientists at Surrey University.

Researchers in the school of biological sciences have triumphed over research teams worldwide in modifying a technique used to analyse and alter DNA extracted from harmful bacteria to produce a strain that no longer causes the disease and also provides protection against it' (Patel, 1995).

Far from being defeated, medicine claims to be working on solutions to what Sir Dai Rees, chief executive of the British Medical Research Council, has described as one of the 'great challenges' (Rees, 1995). The fields of genetics and pharmacology, and now the civilian population, are enlisted in its war of attrition against such diseases as tuberculosis, and the media are ebullient:

'Ten million lives will be saved in new TB strategy. The worldwide battle against tuberculosis is being won ... A recently introduced method of treating the disease, which uses existing drugs but provides strict supervision to ensure that patients take them, meant the TB epidemic was levelling off ... DOTS [directly observed treatment short-course] uses health workers and sometimes volunteers, such as shopkeepers and teachers, to ensure patients take a combination of four medicines over six to eight months' (Mihill, 1997a).

The 'medical imagination' is insuperable, and its spin-doctoring indomitable. The ultimate triumph of conquering all disease is assured. Perhaps more surprisingly, the future viability of the 'new' biomedicine model is something that (some) social scientists are beginning to take seriously. For example, Mike Bury, professor of sociology at London University, appears to take a 'realist' position by arguing that to perceive medicine, biology and genetics merely as socially constructed discourses (and therefore only one way of understanding the world) is to trivialise the scope and effect of the knowledge surging from these disciplines:

'Even the most cursory reading of recent popular writing in the biological sciences, for example that of the evolutionary biologist EO Wilson, or the geneticist Steve Jones, indicates the enormous power of the explanatory models being employed, and the extent of their manipulation of the natural world' (Bury, 1995, p45-6).

Charters

In the early 1990s, the Conservative government in Britain launched a 10-year Charter programme aimed at empowering the individual in her or his dealings with public organisations. The Citizen's Charter, for example, pledged specific output levels for individual services, and where these failed to live up to expectations, customers were offered compensation. There are now more than 42 charters (Nye, 1996), covering national and regional institutions such as primary schools, the police, the postal service, the railways, and local authority car parking and refuse collection.

Although most people have heard of the overall scheme (Nye, 1996), the charter relating to health care (i.e. the Patient's Charter) may have a long way to go before achieving its goals: 'People know little of their rights under the Patient's Charter, a survey for the Royal College of Nursing suggests ... fewer than three in 10 people can identify any of its rights or standards' (Brindle, 1994a).

More fundamentally, however, how can health care users be empowered when medical practitioners have the right to refuse treatment? (Berens, 1995). For example, the Association of Community Health Councils for England and Wales reported on a survey of more than 200 community health councils (Brindle, 1994b). In one year, general practitioners were found to have removed from their lists 30,000 patients.

On a more bizarre note, Mihill (1996) reports on the annual meeting of the British Medical Association's family doctors committee, during which the idea of organising a complaints system against troublesome patients was discussed as a reaction to the upsurge in demands made on general practitioners as a result of the Patient's Charter!

Illman (1991) also questions the reality of the active consumer. He argues that many consumers are not 'active' because they may not know what they need in the first place, do not have the skills or motivation to assess the quality of the service they have received, and most still believe that 'doctor knows best'.

Theory Update

In order to accommodate some of the wider economic and political changes that have occurred over the 20 years since he produced his exposition of the professions, Freidson (1988) has produced a more concise definition of professionalism. Three forms of autonomy have been identified by Elston (1991). The first is 'economic autonomy', which refers to the right of the profession to decide on what remuneration its members will receive. The second is described as 'political autonomy', and relates to the ability of the profession to determine policy on health issues. The third type is 'clinical autonomy', and refers to the right of the profession to regulate its own practice and decide on the content of its work. Freidson counters his critics by arguing that his definition of professionalism does not need to include political and economic autonomy, and therefore:

'The loss of extensive political influence and economic independence does not represent the loss of professionalism as I have defined it ... Neither economic independence nor control of professional institutions independently of the state or of capital is essential to professionalism. What is essential is control over the performance and evaluation of a set of demarcated tasks, sustained by the established jurisdiction over a particular body of knowledge and skill' (Freidson, 1988, p385).

Technical autonomy (which equates to Elston's definition of 'clinical autonomy') is, for Freidson, the *sine qua non* of professionalism. Freidson admits that even with this narrower definition of professionalism (in which there is no mention of domination of related occupations), some threat to technical autonomy has been experienced by medicine. He provides the example of how review committees in the United States have been set up to examine clinical work. Although there is no direct equivalent in Britain, auditing and the emergence of the new occupational group of health economists, with its emphasis on the financial regulation of professional practice, may have a similar effect (Ashmore et al., 1989; Power, 1992).

However, Freidson insists that the professional status of medical practitioners remains intact as long as the work they do is under the control of its own members: 'In the United States, as in most other countries, only members of the profession have the right to establish legitimate and authoritative technical standards for medical work, and only they have the right to exercise authority over the technical conduct of medical work' (Freidson, 1988, p386).

It is, however, Freidson's original depiction of professionalism, with its emphasis on the professional being able to determine extensively 'the content and the terms of work' (1970b, p134), and the 'dominance of its expertise in the division of labour 1970b, p136), that remains applicable today. Medicine remains an occupation with a substantial power base despite contemporary bureaucratic, political, economic and consumerist infringements. Consequently, this version of the professional-dominance thesis provides still the most appropriate theoretical tool to analyse the professions.

Summary

A critical review of the literature on the professions indicates that Freidson's (1970a; 1970b) depiction of a profession as an occupation that has autonomy over an area of work, and dominance over related occupations, is still of relevance as a theoretical tool in the late 20th century. Taking the example of medicine, the literature indicates that there has been some loss of control over resources (because of the introduction of general management to the NHS).

However, despite predictions to the contrary (Gabe et al., 1994), there has not been any significant degree of proletarianisation or deprofessionalisation of medicine. Neither has the threat of competitive ideologies (e.g. from 'alternative' health care), the rise of sophisticated technology, the increase in the codification of knowledge, or the suggested existence of an active consumer, affected the relative power of medicine.

Conversely, it can be argued that some of these contemporary processes and structures have allowed medicine to consolidate its professional status. Moreover, in what could be regarded as a demonstrative irony, a review of NHS managers' and doctors' pay has attested to the far greater earning power of the latter compared with the former: 'Twice as many doctors as managers earn more than £90,000 a year from the NHS, research shows today ... The findings put into context the belief that managers have become the "fat cats" of the NHS' (Brindle, 1997).

Not only is the proposition that the power of doctors has been sequestrated highly questionable, but even if this were the case, they would appear to be compensated admirably!

Chapter 3
Nursing as a Profession

If Freidson's (1970a; 1970b) original account of professionalism (which includes the concepts of clinical autonomy *and* professional dominance) is adopted, then what can be said about the occupation of nursing? That is, is nursing 'essentially a subordinate occupation ... Or is it an autonomous profession like medicine?' (Dingwall, 1986, p27).

Traditionally, the protagonists of the occupational strategy of professionalisation for nursing, and other caring occupations (e.g. occupational therapy and physiotherapy), have adhered to the 'trait' theory of professional identity. That is, they have attempted to assess first what constituents of a profession these groups have already. They have then identified ways in which the absent characteristics can be gained (Wallis, 1987; Atkinson, 1988; Jolley, 1989; Abbott and Wallace, 1990).

Accepting implicitly what Etzioni (1969) describes as the 'quasi-professional' status of the paramedical disciplines, the leaders of, for example, nursing, have pursued the policy of professionalisation in order to achieve what they consider to be the full professional identity and high social status of other occupational groups such as law and medicine.

Rafferty (1996), tracing the history of policy-making in nurse education, observes that the vanguard of nursing policy has been explicitly about the arrogation of schemes cultivated by others. This occurred in the spheres of education, clinical practice and 'professional politics': 'Nurse leaders and policy-makers borrowed ideas and action plans developed by groups and institutions that they perceived as being already successful ... Nurse reformers often adopted strategies pioneered by medical reformers. Indeed medicine's influence upon nursing extended beyond the clinical environment: it provided a model for emulation in the propagation of a populist professional politics' (Rafferty, 1996, p182).

Perceptions of Nursing

Perceptions of nursing vary and are often contradictory. A persistent image is one that stems from the assertion by Nightingale (1859) that nursing is a vocation, with nurses viewed as dedicated to the service of their patients. This was to counteract the prevailing negative image in the early 19th century of nursing as being a service delivered by women at the lowest level of the social strata. Nursing was, therefore, perceived to be akin to the work of prostitutes.

The nurse (female) is also seen as dedicated to the role of hand-maiden to the doctor (male) in the delivery of diagnostic techniques and treatments. This stemmed from the mid-19th century, when the medical profession's engagement with scientific knowledge required reliable assistants to deliver the mundane and routine aspects of medical practice when the doctor was not present (Abel-Smith, 1960). Wainwright, using Ashdown's (1943) ideal typification of the 'good nurse', summarises the conventional approach to nursing:

'By tradition, nursing has been seen as a dependent occupation, the nurse being expected to be the ears and eyes of the doctor, loyally carrying out instructions and faithfully reporting back. A nurse was expected to be "punctual, good tempered, obedient, and loyal to all rules as the foundation of her work". She must also remember "what is due to authority" and "must ever remember that discipline and obedience are the keynote to satisfactory and efficient work in life" ' (Wainwright, in Hunt and Wainwright, 1994, p3).

The nurse, therefore, was to be the doctor's 'good wife' in the workplace, tending to his professional needs. Commenting on the analysis offered by feminist critiques, Turner (1987) suggests that the apparent failure of nursing to become professionalised is in part because it is predominantly female (in terms of the numbers of its members). Added to the problems of bureaucratic control (Davies in Dingwall and Lewis, 1983), the inherent 'masculine' features of bureaucratic administration (Davies, 1996), and the lack of coherent professional representation, are the conflicting demands on the nurse of work and family responsibilities:

'The critical issue in the absence of professional status in the history of nursing has centred on the question of gender. The ultimate failure of nursing to achieve professional autonomy is explained in terms of the contradiction between family life and professional careers, bureaucracy and professionalism, the absence of a continuous commitment to a career to the exclusion of domestic involvements ... Women are exploited as nurses because they are socialised into a doctrine which equates nursing with mothering and sees the hospital ward as merely an extension of the domestic sphere of labour' (Turner, 1987, p149).

For some feminist theorists, the structural nature of patriarchal society affects the division of labour both in the workplace and in health care organisations. At work, the role of the 'wife' is played by the secretary, whereas the nurse plays the role of 'mother' in the hospital (Ehrenreich and English, 1976; Garmarnikow, 1978; Game and Pringle, 1983).

New Nursing

The public perception of nursing retains elements of sexuality and servility. For example, Salvage's (1985) study of lay, media and nurses' opinions registered images of the nurse as an angel and sex symbol, as well as that of a battle-axe. However, Smith (1993) believes that a new image of nursing may be evolving. The emergence of 'new nursing' came about in the 1980s, and had been grasped by the elite elements of nursing (managers, educationalists and policy makers) with great enthusiasm: 'Since 1984 there has been an unprecedented burst of activity in and around nursing in the United Kingdom, culminating in proposals for the reform of various aspects of work and training' (Salvage, 1988, p515).

In part, the new nursing is based on changes in the way nurses are educated. For example, in the 1980s, a radically new syllabus for nurses undergoing state registration was introduced. Furthermore, there has been a huge increase in the percentage of nurses undertaking educational programmes in universities, both for initial training and for post-basic courses (Macleod Clark et al., 1996). By the end of the 20th century, mainly at the behest of NHS-based educational consortia, the majority of formal educational input for nurses will delivered by the university sector.

For Smith, the new image of nursing is concerned also with the separation of nursing from medical work, and with the ritualistic and hierarchical way in which care was delivered in the past:

> 'Hospital nursing was organised around the execution of tasks as part of the medical division of labour ... In the 1960s, task allocation was still strong. The most junior and least experienced nurses undertook tasks perceived as basic or simple, such as dusting the ward furniture or cleaning the bedpans. As the nurse became more senior s/he graduated through a series of tasks from giving bedpans, doing the bed baths, taking the temperatures and blood pressures, and finally the dressings, drug round and injections' (Smith, 1993, pp 209–10).

The new nursing has been underpinned by the production of a conceptual foundation (the 'nursing process'), which had been developed over the previous two decades by nurse theorists such as Henderson (1966). Incorporated within this conceptual foundation is a philosophy of holistic care. Holistic approaches to nursing practice are aimed at including psychological and social factors alongside the physical and biological, as well changing the focus of care delivery from that of treating 'disease' to promoting 'health'.

The philosophy of 'put the patient at the centre of care' (Macleod Clark et al., 1996, p198) – which has its roots in humanistic psychology – has also been espoused as a legitimate ideological base for the new nursing. Here, the identification and satisfaction of the patient's needs ('patient-centredness') are seen as paramount, as opposed to the 'expert-centred' diagnosis and treatment of illness and disease.

One other important element in the new nursing movement is the concept of primary nursing. This concentrates on 'structural and organisational factors such as staff allocation and off-duty rotas which enable continuity of patient allocation' (Wainwright, in Hunt and Wainwright, 1994, p14).

Primary nursing has been encouraged by a government initiative that emphasises the importance of the identity of the particular nurse (and her or his 'associates') who has been given the responsibility for the care of a selected number of patients. The idea is that the quality of care will be improved if patients, whether they are treated in hospital or in the community, know the name of this nurse. Moreover, it is assumed that the nurse will form closer and more helpful relationships with patients if there is a declared commitment to identified individuals.

However, the success of the named-nurse scheme has been called into question. In the Royal College of Nursing survey mentioned above, less than one person in 100 knew anything about the scheme. Furthermore, out of more than 900 people who had been treated by a nurse in the year prior to the study, only 49% said they were aware of being given a named nurse (Brindle, 1994a).

Overall, the emphasis of the new nursing is the attempt to 'redefine the nurse's role in order to assert its unique contribution to healing, the challenging of assumptions about nursing's subordination to medicine, and the idea of replacing a bureaucratic occupation with a profession' (Wainwright, in Hunt and Wainwright, 1994, p3).

When the new nursing movement began, the reaction of medical staff was one of hostility. Smith (1993) records that the introduction of nursing care plans and primary nursing caused an outcry from medical practitioners. For example, numerous letters and editorials in the medical journals referred to the resentment that doctors felt about nurses distancing themselves from their historical ties with the medical profession.

Re-medicalising Nursing

Smith (1993) points out that despite some movement away from (medical) procedures towards care focused on the needs of the patient and controlled by nursing objectives, much of the nurse's work remains shaped and directed by medical imperatives: 'Although the organisation of nursing care in hospitals has become more patient-centred in line with the nursing process, many tasks and routines shaped by medical diagnosis and treatment are still apparent. These tasks and routines include doctor's rounds, diagnostic tests and therapies on and off the ward' (p210).

The desire by nurses to extend their role into more prestigious areas of work (Hunt and Wainwright, 1994) can be viewed as another characteristic of new nursing. For example, the Royal College of Surgeons is examining the possibility of using nurses to compensate for the reduction in the working hours of junior doctors (Muir, 1993). Although nurses may at present indulge covertly in duties within hospital theatres that are considered ordinarily (and legally) to be the specific province of medical practitioners, what is being promoted is an official policy of employing nurses as 'surgeons' assistants'. The proposition followed the apparently successful training of an ex-staff nurse to help in heart by-pass operations. This is an idea borrowed from the United States, where there are approximately 20,000 of these assistants, which requires the nurses to perform simple, routine and repetitive tasks during surgery.

Far from enhancing the status of nursing, however, taking on medical 'dirty work' (Hughes, 1971) reinforces the traditional doctor-nurse relationship. Coinciding with other significant trends in Britain, such as the expansion in the number of nurses working in general practice (which effectively makes the nurse an 'employee' of the family doctor), many nurses have once again an explicit 'handmaiden' role.

To argue that the majority of nurses do not work as surgeons' or general practitioners' assistants, and hence these cases do not represent the norm, is to miss the point that their structural association with medicine allows for this possibility. On the other hand, nurses do 'dominate' medical staff in particular circumstances. For example, junior doctors are often dependent on nursing staff for advice about the 'custom and practice' of new clinical placements. Also there are in existence 'nurse-led' hospital wards, which function without the regular involvement of doctors (Griffiths and Evans, 1995). However, it is inconceivable that doctors could be assistants to nurses on any systematic, prolonged and licit basis. Moreover, in the main, it is the medical profession itself that is calling for nurses to undertake these chores (perhaps inspired by government cost-saving measures), under either the general instructions or direct administration of its own practitioners.

Organisations that represent nurses tend to condone the 'medicalisation' of nursing. For example, the Royal College of Nursing has supported research that recommends that nurses should deal with out-of-hours

telephone calls to family doctors (Cooper, 1996b). Following prescribed guidelines, nurses would provide advice to patients, and a doctor would be summoned if demanded by the patient. Furthermore, the
English National Board for Nursing, Midwifery and Health Visiting
(ENB, 1995) approved a new educational programme concerning
specifically the role of the nurse in medical procedures, the title of
which is 'Nurse as Assistant to the Surgeon'.

External Restraints

The attempt by nurses to shed task-orientated work may be thwarted
also by the pressures on nursing staff to provide a cost-effective service
with a high turnover of patients. Medical commitment to positivistic
and technical science contributes further to this reversal. Stated simply,
patients may not spend enough time in hospital for the nurse to implement those principles of the new nursing that involve holism, care planning, etc., and for the patient to benefit from having a named nurse.
Neither is it likely, because of the resource implications, that the new
nursing can be delivered successfully in the community. Moreover, it is
medicine, responding to the managerial cost-efficiency drives, that has
been at the forefront of the techno-scientific advancements that have
resulted in patients having shorter spells in hospital.

Consequently, the same process that devalues nursing has the effect
of improving the status of medicine. Hart (1991) found that nurses still
display deference to medical practitioners. When nurses talked to doctors they were much less articulate and less outspoken than when they
talked to her. This discrepancy, the nurses explained to Hart, was
because they believed themselves to be inferior to, and of less importance than, the medical staff.

If new nursing can be seen as having failed to change the traditional role of nurses (particularly with reference to their relationship with
doctors), can nursing ever be a profession? Dingwall's position on the
prospect of nursing reaching the same professional status as medicine
is quite clear: 'The practice of ... [nursing] work remains firmly subordinate to that of the doctor. With the exception of health visitors, no
nurse has an independent access to work or its allocation ... The doctor retains the sole control over the focal tasks of diagnosis and treatment. The nurse still requires his authority to penetrate the body physically or chemically ... functional autonomy for any group other than
doctors is, at best, a pipe-dream' (Dingwall, 1974, p53).

Freidson (1970a) is also clear that nursing can never be anything
other than a 'semi-profession'. The knowledge base for nursing
(despite the attempts of the advocates of new nursing) remains within
the remit of the medical model. Furthermore, Freidson argues that as

doctors control the admission of patients, they are ultimately responsible for the diagnosis and treatment, and therefore wield much influence over nursing practice.

Heterogeneity

A number of commentators on the future of nursing as an occupational group have questioned whether professionalisation is a suitable goal for nursing (Dingwall et al., 1988; Salvage, 1988). Melia (1987), for example, has proposed that nursing as a whole could replace the sought elitism of professionalism with the autonomy of the craft worker. It may be that each sub-group of nursing (e.g. child, adult, learning disabilities and mental health) has to develop and implement its own strategy to achieve either full professional status, or attempt to sustain or improve its position in the occupational hierarchy by alternative methods to professionalism.

That is, given that nursing cannot be perceived as an homogeneous collection of workers (Butterworth, 1984; Abbott and Wallace, 1990, p17), as is the case with many other occupational groupings (Bucher and Strauss, 1961; Bucher, 1962), it may not be politically or pragmatically astute for those representing its numerous factions to partake in a unified occupational strategy. A diversification in occupational strategies and goals has already taken place to some extent, and with variable success, for a number of health care groups associated with nursing. For example, Abbott and Sapsford comment on the case of health visiting: 'Health visitors are not unaware of the contradictions and problems of their role position. In recent years these have led them on the one hand to seek professional status and on the other to monitor and evaluate their own work in more detail. They have been led to consider who they are, and what work they ought to be doing' (Abbott and Wallace, 1990, p122).

Health visitors, along with midwives, have claimed independent practitioner status (Dingwall et al., 1988). In doing so, they have attempted to secure their position as aligned with but separate to nursing, and increase their standing as professionals ahead of that achieved by nurses.

This attempt to obtain the status of 'independent practitioner' is characterised by the health care worker being able to carry out her or his practice autonomously. That is, to be able to operate without recourse to medical supervision in practical day-to-day decision making and, at an ideological level, to be free from medical hegemony. It should be emphasised, however, that this is only an 'attempt' by groups such as health visitors and midwives to be independent. The degree of success or self-delusion involved in this quest can be contested (Dingwall et al., 1988; Benoit, 1989; Willis, 1990).

With reference to midwifery, although there has been a growth in the number of independent midwives, doctors have effectively taken over child-birth, mainly because of the hospital confinement of pregnant women. This leaves midwives exposed to medical and bureaucratic domination. Where midwives have attempted to avoid both of these forms of domination (e.g. through the setting up of groups aimed at self-help), they have not necessarily been successful:

> 'Midwives seeking to exercise their role to the full have often been con-
> strained by the bureaucracy surrounding maternity care or by medical con-
> trol to such an extent that some have gone into practice outside traditional
> structures ... These alternative patterns of practice are not always sanc-
> tioned by health care organisers to whom independent practice and/or the
> supporting of women to give birth at home can be seen to undermine the
> dominant mode of operation. Where midwives have formed self-help groups
> they have found it hard for their voices to be heard' (Silverton, in Hunt and
> Wainwright, 1994, p154).

Furthermore, an experiment within the NHS, in which midwives provided every aspect of the maternity service, has proven to be inefficient.
The results from the three pilot studies participating in the research
point to the women receiving the service being very satisfied. But,
because of the cost and the necessary high level of commitment by the
staff, the service will not be replicated nationally (Mihill, 1997b). This
can be interpreted as an abortive attempt by midwifery to sell itself in
the health care market place, and as part of a manoeuvre to be a self-
reliant profession, a serious failure.

As Wainwright (1994) observes, there are contradictory processes at
work in relation to how nurses operate and perceive themselves, and
this has an effect on their occupational status. For example, Wainwright
suggests that at the same time as demanding independence, nurses also
wish to remain 'part of the team'. In doing so, he argues, nurses prolif-
erate conventional relationships:

> 'Nursing is still very much in a transitional state. On the one hand we have
> the development of primary nursing and arguments for autonomy and self-
> governance, reinforced by initiatives such as the named nurse, nurse pre-
> scribing, the development of specialist and advanced practitioners, and the
> reduction of junior doctors' hours ... On the other hand we have, appar-
> ently, a deep desire on the part of many nurses to be part of the team and
> to continue in the *status quo* [emphasis by Wainwright]' (p17).

That is, Wainwright is implying that being a team player has the effect
of nullifying any advancement in independent practice for nurses,
resulting in occupational stagnation rather than elevation.

Furthermore, as with medicine, the introduction of managerialism
into the NHS will influence how much of nursing work can be defined

by either nurses or doctors. Managers, as discussed in the previous section, may enact controls over nursing and medicine that will shift the balance of power, and force both to reconsider their position in the occupational hierarchy.

Although nurses in the future may occupy senior positions among the cadre of NHS managers (Owens and Glennerster, 1990), and possibly further the interests of their discipline, at present they generally hold lower managerial positions. Moreover, new managerialism has imposed structures that are, in the main, more harmful to nursing than to medicine (Baggott, 1994).

Relative Autonomy

For Wainwright (1994), the options for nursing rest on the ability of its members to take on extra responsibilities and thereby extend their role. This will help nurses to 'achieve authority over the nature of their practice' (p19). However, the evidence suggests that nursing, as a whole, is structurally disadvantaged in the hierarchy of health care occupations. Any autonomy gained is only relative to the willingness of general managers, politicians and the profession of medicine to allow it to happen. Nursing does not have the power base of, for example, medicine (which has maintained its professional dominance), and hence this 'relative autonomy' can be reversed at any time.

I have used the term 'relative autonomy' elsewhere, for example, in an analysis of the level of freedom experienced by health care staff undertaking so-called 'student-centred' educational programmes (Morrall, 1989b). It is a concept borrowed from Althusser (1969), who uses it to denote the degree to which the superstructure (e.g. social and cultural institutions, political beliefs, interpersonal and personal behaviour) is free from constraints and pressures of the economic base (e.g. capitalism). I am arguing here that nurses may have freedom in many areas of their working practices to make decisions independent of directives from medical practitioners (or managers), but nursing is shaped ultimately by medical imperatives and ideologies.

Moreover, the intention behind new nursing to 'attenuate medical dominance ... and thus lead to increased occupational status for nursing' (S. Porter, 1996, p75), is severely impaired if less qualified 'generic' support staff are employed instead of nurses. The Health Services Management Unit at Manchester University has recommended such a course of action (Fletcher, 1996). This policy is portrayed as a way of getting round the problem of 'out-of-date' role demarcations in order to provide a flexible (and less expensive) workforce that can meet the needs of service users. It has the support of the management of the health services in the form of the National Association of Health

Authorities and NHS Trusts. However, the general secretary of the Royal College of Nursing responded to its launch by admitting that if it were implemented, it would 'destroy nursing' (Fletcher, 1996), a reaction that demonstrates how vulnerable the discipline of nursing is (compared with that of medicine) to the process of de-professionalisation.

Summary

Nursing is not, and cannot become, a profession, as it has no legitimate ideology, its practice arena is diminishing, and health care assistants are replacing qualified nurses. Furthermore, the work of nursing is becoming 'medicalised' because nurses are accepting such roles as that of surrogate 'junior doctor' and 'surgeon's assistant'. An increase in occupational status of the semi-professions in the health care field was also expected to weaken the dominant position of medicine. However, in the case of nursing, not only has this not happened, but it may be that this occupational group is experiencing a reversal of any independence from medicine it could claim to have achieved.

The next question to be addressed is, has mental health nursing disentangled itself from the rest of nursing and achieved (or has it the potential to achieve) a professional status?

Chapter 4
Mental Health Nursing

Following the application of Freidson's (1970a; 1970b) perspective to review both medicine and nursing as a whole, in this chapter his approach is employed to evaluate the literature on mental health nursing. As with medicine and nursing, the notions of clinical autonomy and professional dominance are used as focal points.

The question being asked here is, do mental health nurses have control over their clinical practice? That is, can they define the content and limit of their labour? If they have this control, then they could be viewed as having moved substantially in the direction of professionalisation. However, if the literature indicates that the management of their work is susceptible to the dominance and hegemony of other health care professionals (e.g. medicine), then psychiatric nursing can be described only as a subordinate occupational group. It can be regarded as remaining under the occupational umbrella of nursing as a whole, having the status of, in Freidson's terminology, a 'paramedical' profession.

Psychiatric nurses working in the community are susceptible to a greater degree of freedom than 'institutional' nurses. Therefore, the position of community psychiatric nursing, and the present situation of the CPN in the multidisciplinary team, is reviewed in detail. Empirical evidence from my research study of clinical independence among CPNs is provided in subsequent chapters.

Mental Health Nursing

There are more than 57,000 psychiatric nurses working in the NHS, and they form the largest group of mental health workers (Sainsbury Centre 1997). Peplau (1994) observes that the development of mental health nursing 'has coincided with changes in psychiatric care' (p3). To put it more strongly, the role played by mental nurses cannot be separated from both the immediate and the wider social contexts (e.g. local and national political decisions and economic policies) affecting the care of the mentally ill. In particular, the existence and performance of psychiatric nursing is indivisible from the historical interest of the medical profession in expanding its sphere of influence over the treatment of the mad, and is entangled inescapably with the social control function of psychiatry.

Nolan (1993) records that the history of mental health nursing can be traced back to the keeper of the various types of 'houses' in which mad people lived before the 1845 Lunacy Act. Accommodation for the sick was known to exist in the ancient world. The treatment provided by these institutions was governed by the religious context in which they were often situated.

In Britain, however, there is some doubt as to whether hospitals existed before the 10th century (Cartwright, 1977). Apart from the 'lazar house', which assisted people suffering from leprosy, the purpose of a hospital at this time was not defined clearly: 'It could be a geriatric unit, an orphanage, a reformatory for unmarried mothers, a rest house for travellers, an infirmary for the sick, or much more frequently, it could serve all these purposes' (Cartwright, 1977, p30).

By the 15th century, special provision for the mad was being created. As Cartwright (1977, p31) notes, in the mid-1400s 'Bedlam' offered sanctuary for 'many men that have fallen out of their wits'. Until the beginning of the 19th century, the mad were mostly still cared for by their families (Scull, 1993). However, thousands of mentally disordered people were contained, from the 17th century onwards, within houses of correction, private madhouses and local parish workhouses. They were victims of the pan-European 'Great Confinement' (Foucault, 1967), which resulted in those who challenged the moral values of the bourgeois class being isolated from the rest of the population. These 'deviant' groups included the poor, the work-shy, the homeless and criminals. In Foucault's (1967) terms, 'reason' was separated from 'unreason'.

Following the 1845 Lunacy Act, local authorities were forced to provide for the mad through a massive public building programme. Along with the Poor Law Amendment Act 1834, the 1845 act heralded the beginning of 'Victorian Asylumdom' – the segregation of the mad into a centralised and unitary form of residence away from the rest of the community and other deviant populations (Foucault, 1967; Scull, 1979, 1993). This first 'psychiatric revolution' (Scull, 1981) presented the opportunity for the profession of medicine, and therefore also nursing, to emerge as legitimate 'surveyors' of the mad. That is, the medical profession was not instrumental in the creation of the asylum movement, but capitalised on a captive population that reached 100,000 by 1900:

'The sequestration of lunatics was primarily an expression of civil policy, more an initiative from magistrates, philanthropists and families than an

achievement – for good or ill – of the doctors. Indeed, the rise of psychological medicine was more the consequence than the cause of the rise of the
insane asylum. Psychiatry could flourish once, but not before, large numbers
of inmates were crowded into asylums' (Porter, 1987, p17).

From the late part of the 18th century, 'moral treatment', supported by
lay philanthropists and religious groups such as the Quakers, compet-
ed with the stimulants, sedatives, emetics, purgatives, bloodletting,
cold and hot baths, mechanical restraints and electric shocks, of 'organic' psychiatry.

Moral management invoked a kinder approach, which held that the
mad could be brought back to reason if handled more humanely:

'This movement aimed in effect to revive the dormant humanity of the mad,
by treating them as endowed with a residuum at least of normal emotions,
still capable of excitation and training ... They needed to be treated essentially like children, who required a stiff dose of rigorous discipline, rectifica-
tion and retraining in thinking and training' (Porter, 1987, p19).

However, in the early 19th century, the medical profession succeeded
in preventing the protagonists of this movement from gaining legal control over the asylums. Employing a technique that has served the profession of medicine extremely well, rather than deriding this popular
approach, doctors encompassed moral therapy within their assortment
of procedures. The effect of 'medicalising' moral treatment was to leave
psychiatrists 'in charge of the whole enterprise' (Johnstone, 1989,
p177).

By the time the 1890 Lunacy Act was instituted, the profession of
medicine had monopolised the market with regard to the care of the
mad, and this resulted in the redefining of the category of 'madness' to
one of 'mental illness' (Baruch and Treacher, 1978). After 1845, the
keeper changed into the 'attendant'. The attendants were responsible
for the general upkeep of the new institutions for the insane, but were
to become 'the medical superintendent's servants, with primary
responsibility to carry out his orders' (Nolan, 1993, p6). Women who
became attendants were referred to as 'nurses'. It was not until the end
of the 19th century that men were also accorded this title.

For Nolan (1990), the creation of a Register for Attendants under the
1890 Act marks the start of the formal recognition of the occupation of
psychiatric nursing. The title 'mental nurse' was inaugurated in the
General Council's Supplementary Register for Mental Nurses of 1923
(Nolan, 1993).

However, the history of psychiatric nursing, because of its association with the geographically isolated 'asylum', is very different to that of
general nursing. Moreover, because of its origins, psychiatric nurses can
be viewed as having been more receptive to medical dominance than

other nurses. For example, the social class divide between psychiatrists and mental health nurses has been much greater than that between doctors and nurses in the general field.

Employment in the asylum was poorly rewarded as it demanded that attendants 'tolerate the defiling close daily contact with the derelict' (Scull, 1993, p173). Therefore, although recruitment into general nursing was mainly from the middle class, asylum attendants and psychiatric nurses historically have been drawn from the working class, or the unemployed. This produced a greater 'us' and 'them' divide between nurses and doctors working in mental health, than between their counterparts in general medicine.

Furthermore, psychiatric nurses have had less commitment to the occupational goal of nursing: 'The ideology of professionalism with its sporadic appeals, that the nursing of the insane required both "high calling" and "the best qualities of the heart and head", cut little ice with asylum workers. They had a class consciousness similar to that of other manual occupations and required remuneration for their main means of subsistence' (Rogers and Pilgrim, 1996, p108).

More significantly, medical practitioners had established themselves as administrators of the asylum to a far greater degree than their colleagues in the general hospital. Furthermore, the medical superintendent, as the senior administrator of the asylum (and later the mental hospital), was omnipotent and ubiquitous in the lives of the nursing staff. Attendants in the asylum were supervised closely to ensure 'a measure of conformity from such an ill-suited lot' (Scull, 1993, p173). Asylum nurses, in comparison with general nurses, could be discharged for relatively trivial misdemeanours, and the 'rules' of the medical superintendent applied whether they were working or off-duty: 'Asylum rule-books meant that such things as "disobedience of elders" or intemperance (even outside the asylum) were grounds for instant dismissal' (Rogers and Pilgrim, 1996, p109).

The influence of medicine on mental nursing was maintained throughout the 19th and a large proportion of the 20th centuries. Any gains made by nursing to assert itself as a discrete discipline were undermined in the 1930s and 1940s when more physical treatments (for example, psychosurgery and insulin therapy) were introduced. In the 1950s, the discovery of anti-psychotic drug treatments and their success in stabilising such conditions as schizophrenia, reaffirmed the biomedical base for the treatment of mental illness.

This had the consequence of focusing nursing practice on pharmaceutical routines and rituals, instigated by medical practitioners, with the mental nurse ordained as the 'therapeutic technician' to the psychiatrist (Prior, 1993). The 'drug round' became the most important task in the nurse's working day, symbolising the hallowed mystique of the medical profession. Tablets and syrups had to be measured by a 'senior' nurse. Student nurses were trained in the use, side effects, handling and storage of these drugs, as well as how to deal with patients who refused to take their medication. Equipment (e.g. the drug trolley) was liable to special cleansing. Although nurses could use their clinical judgement to a minor degree, ultimately, the prescribing, alteration of dosages and discontinuation of drug regimes was controlled by the doctor. The drama of the drug-giving performance scripted nurses as ecclesiastic acolytes, doctors as hierophants and patients as the participating congregation.

It was only after 1982, with the introduction of a new syllabus, that nurses were formally expected to be aware of a wide range of social and psychological factors in the causation and treatment of mental distress. Training for registered mental nurses now included, for example, interpersonal and counselling skills. Moreover, previously taboo subjects, such as the patient's 'sexuality', could be studied in nursing texts (Dexter and Wash, 1986).

In the search for an occupational identity, mental health nursing, like health visiting and midwifery, attempted to project itself as a profession: 'Psychiatric nurs[ing] … has, for the last decade, been engaged in strategies to move from being a semiprofession to a fully autonomous profession' (Pilgrim and Rogers, 1993, p149).

However, not long after the introduction of the 1982 syllabus, mental nursing was to go through another major crisis in its occupational identity because of a radical change in the way in which the whole of nurse training was organised (Dingwall et al., 1988). Nurses with an interest in mental health are now educated alongside general nurses for the first time, following a 'common foundation programme' for the first half of their course. Dingwall et al. (1988) have observed that this may leave mental nursing merely as a post-basic speciality.

Another factor causing this crisis for these authors has been the encroachment on mental nurses' work from both social work and psychology. However, as has been mentioned earlier, this can work in reverse, particularly when a discipline such as psychology becomes too expensive in comparison with that of nursing.

Today, psychiatric nursing in Britain is confronted by a multitude of external determinants. These include: the prolonged period of fiscal restraint, inaugurated by a succession of conservative governments (but likely to continue under a labour government), which has meant a significant reduction in state expenditure on public services; the possibility of a reversal of the policy of decarcerating the mentally ill in the light of unabated criticism of care in the community; and the production of yet more official reports attempting to clarify the role of the mental health nurse.

Community Psychiatric Nursing

Community psychiatric nursing, a sub-division of mental health nursing, has a relatively short history. But the importance of CPNs in the mental health field leads Armstrong (1987) to claim that they are, the 'frontline workers of psychiatric care' (p4).

The community aspect of psychiatric nursing can be traced back to 1954 when two nurses were seconded from a mental hospital in Surrey to work as 'out-patient nurses' because of a shortage of social workers. Their role was to keep contact with discharged patients, and to help maintain these patients in the community (May, 1965; Greene, 1968; Hunter, 1974; Sladden, 1979; Carr et al., 1980). Godin makes the point that the development of community psychiatric nursing is connected specifically to the policy of community care, and the need for psychiatrists to have 'eyes and ears' to survey and control (through, for example, medication) the behaviour of patients who had been placed in the public domain:

> 'Psychiatrists' clientele were now increasingly outside the mental hospital. CPNs were seen by psychiatrists as a useful para-professional group that could observe patients in their own homes and administer medication ... CPNs were to psychiatrists a technology by which they could extend their authority beyond the confines of the hospital' (Godin, 1996, p930).

Since then the CPN service has grown considerably, and is continuing to expand. In 1985, there were 3,000 CPNs in the UK and, in 1990, nearly 5,000 (White, 1993; Rogers and Pilgrim, 1996). By the year 2000, it has been projected that 12,500 psychiatric nurses will be community based (CPNA, 1985).

In the 1980s, the role of the CPN is reported to have expanded to include: formal and informal assessment of the client's mental state; the implementation of preventative, educational, and specific therapy programmes; and supportive visits (Beard, 1980; Carr et al., 1980; Williamson et al., 1981). Other aspects of the CPN's role are stated to be the provision of a consultative service to other health-related and voluntary agencies, the provision of physical care and the giving of injections (Mangen and Griffith, 1982; Barratt, 1989). The growth of community psychiatric nursing, however, has been piecemeal and uncoordinated. Pollock (1986a) states: 'Surveys (CPNA 1981 and 1985) ... suggest that CPNing service development is of a local nature and *ad hoc* in character ... CPNing appears to share with other British social and health services a common history of isolated experimental development ... there is great diversity ... in the therapeutic settings in which CPNs work and in the forms of intervention offered by CPNs' (p11).

Throughout its history, community psychiatric nursing has tried to produce an identity that is not only separate from nursing generally, but is also distinct from 'institutional' mental nursing. This is displayed, for example, in the assertion by CPNs that they function (unlike their hospital counterparts) as autonomous practitioners, or have the capacity to do so. An account by Hally of her day's work as a community psychiatric nurse illustrates this. Making the distinction between community psychiatric nursing and all other areas of nursing, she proclaims that the CPN 'is a community mental health worker who is an autonomous practitioner ... there is no other branch of nursing which offers the variety, the challenge, the autonomy and the satisfaction of community psychiatric nursing' (Hally, 1989, p6).

Such an assertion of 'autonomy' and 'satisfaction' may be regarded as self-serving propaganda, an attempt by assentors of community psychiatric nursing to elevate the discipline beyond its actual position in the occupational hierarchy.

Indeed, there is quite a tradition in the peddling of self-congratulatory slogans by those who have supported the CPN movement. For example, Professor Ted White of Keele University, a former CPN educationalist, has described community psychiatric nursing as 'the most important single profession in the process of moving the care of mental illness into the community' (White, 1990, p197).

But it is not only the CPNs and their supporters who proclaim they are well endowed with respect to clinical independence. Johnstone is an ardent critic of psychiatric medicine and nursing. She accepts, however, that although community psychiatric nursing has faced opposition (most obviously from psychiatry) it has been able to constitute itself as a 'fairly independent profession' (Johnstone, 1989, p158). For Johnstone, this achievement is linked directly to CPNs receiving patients from general practitioners. This allows CPNs to take more control over their caseloads than would be feasible if psychiatrists were the main or single group of referrers.

Savio (in Brooker and White, 1995) reports on a comparative study of British and Italian community psychiatric nursing. She argues that the first stage of professionalism must be the procurement of mandatory qualifications. For Savio, educational credentials will help nursing to be distinguished from other disciplines within the mental health 'professional market'. This will, posits Savio, augment nurses' self-identity and lead to increased autonomy. Although mandatory courses for mental health nurses working in the community have yet to be introduced, there is an abundance of educational programmes available. To date, the most pertinent of these has been the post-basic ENB qualification in community psychiatric nursing. The aim of this course, contained in the document of its outline syllabus, makes explicit the connection between educational credentialism and autonomy: 'To produce a practitioner, beyond initial training as a Registered Mental Nurse, who is able to function *autonomously*' [my emphasis] (English National Board, 1989a, p1).

There is, therefore, the assumption that a Registered Mental Nurse does not operate autonomously (at least while working in the community) until this course is undertaken. However, there is the implication that autonomy is achievable.

The aim of this course makes reference not only to the autonomy of the CPN, but also to her or his membership of the multidisciplinary team. As Dean (1988) has observed in her study of Community Mental Health Teams (CMHTs), however, tensions exist between the autonomy of mental health practitioners and team membership (some of which are examined in later chapters).

Foucault (1967) and Scull (1979; 1993) illustrate in their critiques of the origins of the profession of psychiatry and the construction of madness as a medical category, that psychiatrists have dominated other mental health workers since the birth of the asylum. However, 'psychiatric imperialism' may have been tempered by the development of community care, and the running down and closure of the asylums. Conversely, new organisational structures, such as the CMHT, have the potential to alter fundamentally the relationship between the psychiatrist and other mental health workers in the opposite direction. Whether or not the team members physically share one site (for example, in a community mental health centre: CMHC) or function from disparate locations, there is the probability of change occurring to the role behaviour of the various occupational groups (Sheppard, 1991).

Murphy (1991) believes that psychiatrists have indeed lost the leadership of the occupations involved in mental health. But the advent of the CMHT offers psychiatrists the opportunity to reassert their influence over these other mental health disciplines. That is, the CMHT may provide the venue for medical practitioners to regain their leadership role (Bean and Mounser, 1993).

The accomplishment of autonomous practice for nursing has been, in general, measured against how far removed the CPN is from domination by psychiatrists. For example, Simpson (1988), in an article on the subject of CPN autonomy and medical hegemony, perceives the medical profession as restricting the CPNs' access to a particular group of clients:

'CPNs increasingly regard themselves as autonomous practitioners, especially when working with those who are experiencing disabling mental health problems but who cannot be considered mentally ill. But how can autonomy operate when another profession controls access to, and assessment of, this group of clients?' (p5).

Simpson provides evidence justifying professional status for CPNs from an account of one CPN who worked with a group of London general practitioners. Over a period of three years, the CPN assessed and treated, or referred to another health practitioner, 600 clients. The CPN adopted a variety of 'non-medical' approaches and produced a dramatic reduction in the prescription of psychotropic drugs together with a large decrease in hospital referrals.

Simpson believes this case supports the quest of CPNs for autonomous practitioner status. It may also be an example of what Rose (in Miller and Rose, 1986) suggests is 'a new distribution of professional powers'. Rose detracts from the radical criticism of psychiatry which perceives the mental health industry as dominated by positivistic biomedical approaches. Like Clare (1976), he accepts that psychiatry is eclectic in practice, but argues also that non-medical personnel (including nurses) play key roles in the delivery of treatment to the mentally ill: 'There has been no simple medical monopolisation of mental distress, but rather the development of a *free market of expertise*' [Rose's emphasis] (Rose, 1986, p83).

Alternatively, it could be argued that the CPN in Simpson's example was working under licence, and that if the CPN undermined the ultimate authority of medicine, this liberty would be revoked. As White's (1986) research has illustrated, direct access by CPNs to clients continues to be restricted by medical practitioners.

In a further study by White (1990), a postal survey was conducted of all the district health authorities in England. The results indicate that the proportion of referrals received by the CPNs from consultant psychiatrists had halved over the previous 10 years. This, according to White, is a consequence of the closer ties between CPNs and general practitioners.

Following these earlier studies, White (1993) conducted a comprehensive survey of CPNs in England. He reported that 25% of CPNs did not have one client on their caseloads with the diagnosis of schizophrenia. That is, the trend appears to be for CPNs to concentrate more and more on working with clients with minor mental illness at the expense of those with serious mental illness.

Certainly, psychiatrists have been reported to be troubled about the possibility of their monopoly over mental health care being challenged because of the closure of the hospitals, and nurses forming stronger links with Primary Health Care Teams (PHCTs): 'Many psychiatrists are doubtful about, or even openly hostile to the developments' (Sturt and Waters, 1985, p507).

It is worth underlining, however, that both general practitioners and psychiatrists belong to the profession of medicine. Consequently, whether referrals are controlled by general practitioners or by psychiatrists, community psychiatric nursing remains structurally in a subservient relationship with medicine.

Many of the advocates of professionalisation for community psychiatric nursing believe, however, that CPNs are in a unique situation. It could be argued, for example, that the physical location of the practice of community psychiatric nursing (i.e. in the community) presents its members with a greater opportunity to be autonomous than hospital-based nurses. That is, the policy of decarcerating the mentally ill from institutions into the community (Scull, 1983; 1984; Bean and Mounser, 1993) has restructured the work of the nurse, resulting in a greater degree of freedom from the control of both the nursing hierarchy and medicine.

As Freidson observes: 'The nurse, whose leaders in the United States and abroad have with great energy sought to establish unique skills and full professional status, seems fated to remain subject to the doctor's orders in part because of the fact that her work is largely carried out in the hospital' (1988, p57).

Like health visitors, community midwives and, to a lesser extent, district nurses, CPNs work unobserved by medical and other colleagues (as well as their managers) for much of the time. However, Freidson points out the paradox for nursing with respect to its association with medicine and its occupational status: 'Interestingly enough, it appears that *in order to* [Freidson's emphasis] attain semi-professional status, the nurse had to become part of the subordinate paramedical division of labor, and so handicap her chance for subsequent professional status' (1988).

That is, the occupational position of nursing (and in many respects its *raison d'être*) is dependent on linkage with the medical profession. Complete separation of the two occupations might cause nursing to lose even its 'semi' professional prestige, or possibly lead to its complete disintegration as an occupational category.

Community Teams

As has been noted by Hughes (1988), situational differences for the nurse can affect the degree to which she or he exercises autonomy and is free from the domination of others (in particular, the medical staff). CPNs at present operate from any one of a number of geographical sites. Traditionally, they have been housed within the grounds of the psychiatric hospital. Many CPNs moved into the psychiatric units of district general hospitals during the 1970s, and into health centres as either full-time or part-time members of the primary health care team (Sheppard, 1991).

But there remains disagreement as to where, ideally, CPNs should be located. Some argue for CPNs to remain hospital based (Leopoldt, 1979), whereas others have encouraged the movement into primary health care teams (Mangen and Griffith, 1982; Brooker and Simmons, 1985).

A fairly recent innovation has been the creation of the CMHT, which in many cases function from community-based centres (CMHCs). CMHT membership consists of, for example, psychiatric nurses, psychiatrists, psychologists, social workers and occupational therapists (Dean, 1988; Øvretveit, 1993). The development of CMHTs and CMHCs in Britain was influenced by experiments in both the USA and Italy (Sayce et al., 1991). In the USA, these institutional changes to the delivery of care for the mentally ill were supported by legislation (i.e. Community Mental Health Centre Act, passed by Congress in 1963). The aim of the CMHCs was to offer local, accessible, free and universal mental health services (Sayce, 1989).

Cohen (1988) observes that some social commentators have suggested that medical hegemony has been challenged by the creation of CMHCs in the United States. However, Greer and Greer (1984) note that the mental health movement, which had advocated de-institutionalisation and the 1963 Act, gained its intellectual leadership 'from a new professional group, *community psychiatrists*' [my emphasis] (p403). That is, the CMHTs in the USA, rather than challenging medicine, may have provided an occupational territory for a new breed of medical practitioners!

Despite the inappropriateness of importing structures without acknowledging the historical, cultural and political context in which they were developed (Mollica, 1980), CMHCs started to emerge in Britain in the 1970s (Sayce, 1989). The number of CMHCs had grown in the late 1980s from 50 to 230 (Patmore and Weaver, 1989) and, by the mid-1990s, most community mental health practitioners operated within CMHTs (Rogers and Pilgrim, 1996).

This development is encouraged by Wooff and Goldberg: 'There is general acceptance of the view that a multidisciplinary team will provide a better standard of mental-health care than that provided by a single professional working alone' (1988, p36).

Simpson (1986) accepts that the Social Services Committee (1985), and the Cumberlege Report (1986), 'places CPNs firmly in the grip of the multi-disciplinary team' (p7). However, Simpson goes on to point out that the Cumberlege Report also argues that CPN attachment to primary health care teams or nursing services is a 'welcome trend'. Certainly, general practitioners appear to support the inclusion of CPNs in the PHCT (Robertson and Scott, 1985; White, 1986). Pollock, however, like Wooff and Goldberg (1988), questions whether CPNs should work in isolation:

'The community psychiatric nurses themselves may not be the best people to comment impartially on their contribution in relation to individual patients ... it could be proposed that decisions by the community psychiatric nurses about who is treated may be more appropriately taken at a multidisciplinary level, where combined views of different professions can be brought to bear on the work of community psychiatric nurses' (Pollock, 1989, p196).

It is the role of the CPN in primary prevention that appears to give rise to much criticism. For example, it is argued that the CPN's concentration on this area of work, and her or his individualistic and unsupervised style when working with clients who are referred directly from the PHCT, has resulted in a lack of attention being given to the chronically mentally ill (Petroyiannaki and Raymond, 1978; White, 1987; Simmons, 1988; Wooff and Goldberg, 1988).

However, the development of community psychiatric nursing can be seen as surrounded by occupational conflict between CPNs and other mental health professionals (Dean, 1988). Rather than the issue here being about appropriate or inappropriate role-function, much of the criticism about CPNs treating the 'wrong' client group may emanate from their entry into areas of work considered to belong to their colleagues in other disciplines. Therefore, the call for the supervision and better management of CPNs (Wooff and Goldberg, 1988) may turn out to be a strategy to reaffirm dominance over a workforce perceived to be subservient. It is possible, of course, that the CPN may shift eventually from servicing the doctor to servicing the social worker or the psychologist. Alternatively, the CMHT as a whole, acting as 'corporate-preceptor', may become the focal point in the regulation of the CPN's work.

Carr et al. (1980) and Beard (1980) have suggested that the role of the CPN has moved far beyond that of medical adjunct, but even so, as Rogers and Pilgrim (1996) note, CPNs remain affected by interprofessional defensiveness and rivalry.

Commenting specifically on interdisciplinary work in CMHCs, Noon (1988) suggests that a fundamental issue is that of 'collaboration' between the various occupational groups. Using a model proposed by Kane (1975), Noon describes two types of interdisciplinary teams. The first is the 'coordinate team' in which all of the disciplines are considered important to the overall rehabilitation of the patient. However, each discipline tends to enter the situation at a different time, and has a rather specialised role to perform. Most significantly, with the coordinate team, the physician remains the 'leader'.

The second type of team is the 'integrative team'. Here decisions are shared, roles overlap, and there is a shift from focusing on 'leadership' towards an awareness of the effectiveness of team group processes.

The idea that an integrative form of team does (or could) exist in the mental health field may well be idealistic, to say the least. As Noon explains: 'Professional boundaries may be a problem. This includes the question of who is a legitimate member of the team and what the boundaries are between each discipline' (1988, pp1160-1).

Simmons (1988) recognises that working in a team imposes a set of structurally organised role-relationships on the CPN: 'One of the main issues is surely that of leadership. We can espouse many wonderful and idealistic notions about how a team should work collectively with mutually agreed goals, shared or flexible leadership, and genuine blurring and overlapping roles. The reality is, however, often rather different' (p16).

The issue of leadership is one that is not resolved. Consultant psychiatrists have voiced their opinion that they believe they are the natural leaders of multidisciplinary teams (Black and John, 1986; White, 1990). Others (e.g. psychologists) believe the CMHT offers the opportunity to break the psychiatrists' ideological and operational stranglehold over mental health care (Johnstone, 1989). A further structural element is acknowledged by Simmons when she asks whether referrals will be made only through the CMHT. She is concerned that as CPNs are the largest group within the CMHT, they will be expected to 'take on the work which is seen as the least rewarding and prestigious – work with long-term clients with major psychiatric illness' (1988).

There are indications that this will be the case. This pattern of doctors off-loading work on to nurses in general has already been commented on by Dingwall (1974). With reference to CPNs, White (1986) and Dean (1988) identified a strong element of delegation, and a perception of 'subordinate status' by the medical members of the PHCT. With regard to CMHTs, however, Dean states optimistically that: 'The multidisciplinary team approach would seem to offer a potential resolution of the observed misunderstandings between professional groups despite the potential problems of leadership and collegiality' (1988, p335).

But, as Simmons (1988) and Noon (1988) have implied, CPNs may find that this relative freedom is curtailed if they join CMHTs. That is, there is a contradiction in trying to achieve autonomy and at the same time being a member of the CMHT: 'Practitioners used to working independently find that they have less autonomy in a team ... some team members raise "lack of autonomy" as a problem' (Øvretveit, 1993, p116).

Simpson (1986) also spells out the ambiguous situation CPNs can find themselves in, with reference to levels of autonomy, when they belong to a CMHT: 'While there are clear advantages to working in a multidisciplinary team ... there are also great benefits in becoming an autonomous practitioner' (p9).

CMHT membership, therefore, for the CPN (as well as for other occupational groups in the team) may dilute any claim to clinical autonomy, and may consequently reverse any advancement made in the direction of professionalisation.

Multidisciplinary work in the community has been encouraged by various reports and government legislation. These include the 1983

Mental Health Act (DoHWO, 1983), the revised 'Mental Health Act Code of Practice' (DoHWO, 1993) and 'Community care: agenda for action' (Griffiths, 1988).

The nature of team work in the community, however, is about to change again. Further government reforms have had either a direct or indirect effect on interdisciplinary and inter-agency relationships (DoH, 1989a; 1989b; 1990a; 1990b; 1997). These reforms have seen the development of market conditions in the NHS and local authorities, the setting up of NHS Trusts, the separation of providers of services from the purchasers, and the creation of 'fund-holding' in general practice.

But more important, with respect to the role of the CPN, has been the dividing of 'health' and 'social' care in the community, and the implementation of 'care management' (Øvretveit, 1993; Watson, 1994). White and Brooker (1990) suggest that these reforms may cause CPNs to concentrate more on working with the chronically mentally ill rather than the 'worried well', and reduce their involvement with general practitioners. The reforms may also, they believe, underscore the primacy of the consultant psychiatrist in the division of labour of mental heath workers.

Certainly, there remains strong support for CPNs to focus their energies on caring for those with enduring mental illness. For example, this was a conclusion from the Report of the Mental Health Nursing Review Team (DoH, 1994b). Moreover, Gournay (1994) argues that CPNs should be medically directed 'case managers' for people suffering from schizophrenia.

Furthermore, there has been a prolonged debate over recommendations from the Royal College of Psychiatrists for the introduction of 'Community Supervision Orders' (Bean, 1993; Brindle, 1993a; 1993b). The result has been the introduction of 'supervision registers' (NHSME, 1994), as well as 'supervised discharge' under the 1995 Mental Health (Patients in the Community) Act. This has major implications for the position of psychiatric nursing in the occupational hierarchy. For example, under this legislation, CPNs are likely to emerge as 'key workers' in overseeing patients who are to be supervised. This would necessitate CPNs working much more closely with consultant psychiatrists, as well as cause a redefinition of their role. That is, they would become more overtly 'agents of social control'.

Summary

I have argued in this and preceding chapters that nursing as a whole, including (and perhaps especially) mental health nursing, remains a subordinate occupation. Mental health nursing, because of its historical foundations, is linked also to the social control function performed by psychiatry.

Community psychiatric nursing has the potential to obtain a greater degree of freedom because of the 'nature of their work' (Fahy, 1994, p48). However, at present, the literature does not confirm that community psychiatric nursing has achieved a level of clinical autonomy and occupational independence from other professions (particularly medicine), that would indicate it is becoming professionalised. Indeed, the literature implies that CPNs are in a vulnerable position as far as their present status is concerned, and that membership of multidisciplinary teams could jeopardise their self-proclaimed wish for occupational advancement through the strategy of professionalisation.

Chapter 5
Case Study:
Project Design

In the next three chapters, empirical evidence from my study of CPNs is presented as a case study of the professional status of mental health nursing (Morrall, 1995a). The previous chapters serve as a critical review of the literature for the study. In this chapter, the research design of the project is described.

As I have argued in the preceding chapters, according to Freidson, the main method by which medicine and other professions attain high status is through the acquisition of discrete areas of work and by gaining a socially and legally recognised right to work autonomously. That is, people who are considered to belong to a profession 'have the special privilege of freedom from the control of outsiders' (Freidson, 1988, p137). The power of the medical profession depends on a large amount of autonomy over clinical work. In the study reported here, it is Freidson's depiction of professionalism, with his emphasis on the professional being able to determine extensively 'the content and the terms of work' (1970b, p134), that is employed to assess the occupational status of CPNs.

The focus of the research was directed towards identifying the levels of clinical autonomy experienced by psychiatric nurses working in Community Mental Health Teams (CMHTs). Specifically, the study examined the working practices of 10 psychiatric nurses operating as members of four CMHTs in northern England. Apart from the CPNs, the membership of the teams consisted of social workers, psychologists, occupational therapists and consultant psychiatrists. The evaluation of the CPNs' levels of clinical autonomy was achieved by monitoring the referral process (and the decision-making processes) from the stage when new clients were referred to the CPN to when they were discharged, or re-referred to another health care professional. Where clients were not discharged or referred (i.e. treatment by the CPN continued), the collection of data stopped after three months. Questions relevant to these processes include:

1. Does the system of referring clients indicate that the CPNs have clinical autonomy?
2. Do the CPNs have autonomy over their decisions once a client is referred to them?

The professional status of the CPNs was assessed further by examining the opinions of their colleagues in the CMHTs and the managers to whom the CPNs were directly accountable. Relevant questions with regard to how the CPNs' colleagues and managers view the CPNs include:

1. What are the opinions of the members of the CMHT and the managers about the knowledge and skills of the CPN?
2. Is there any interdisciplinary conflict or hierarchy within the CMHT?

These questions provide the basis for the subsequent aims of the research.

Aims of the Study

The aims of the research have been formulated after considering the research problem, the relevant literature and the insights gained during the pre-piloting and piloting of the study. In turn, the aims provided the essence of the questions and probes used in the research tools. There are two aims, each with five sub-aims:

Aim 1: To evaluate the level of clinical autonomy the CPN exercises over the referral process.

Sub-aims: (a) To assess what expectations the referral agents have of the CPN with respect to, for example, the delivery of treatment and to ascertain whether or not these expectations are carried out.

(b) To describe the reasons given by the CPN for accepting referrals.

(c) To examine the methods by which the CPN organises her or his case load.

(d) To identify the degree of conferment and negotiation undertaken by the community psychiatric nurse with, for example, colleagues in the CMHT, general practitioners, supervisors and managers.

(e) To examine the processes used by the CPN when deciding to discharge a client from her or his case load, or to have a client admitted to in-patient psychiatric care.

Aim 2: To analyse ideological and structural influences on the practice of the CPN working within the CMHT.

Sub-aims: (a) To identify systems of belief that affect the CPN's practice.

(b) To describe the meaning of 'team membership' for the CPNs and their colleagues in the CMHT.

(c) To identify systems of supervision and the degree of managerial control over the practice of the CPN.

(d) To establish the existence of any interdisciplinary hierarchy or conflict within the CMHT.

(e) To review the opinions of the CPNs' managers and colleagues in the CMHT with regard to the role and status of the psychiatric nurse working in the community.

The aims presented here are a final version. They are the product of the process of 'reflexivity' (Adler and Adler, 1987). That is, the aims were subject to ongoing reflexive feedback. This resulted in evolutionary and incremental modification as the project unfolded.

All social research is unavoidably subject to the influence of the researcher, the socio-political environment in which studies are conducted and the ideas that occur to the investigator along the route of collecting data: 'We cannot avoid ... having an effect on the social phenomena we study ... there is no way in which we can escape the social world in order to study it' (Hammersley and Atkinson, 1995).

Therefore, the implementation of any research design becomes a 'dynamic' procedure. This does not mean, however, that those undertaking empirical studies in the social arena should disregard their responsibility to produce cogent knowledge, through, for example, being alert for 'the researcher effect' and attempting to install principles of validity and reliability. The notion of 'reflexivity' merely acknowledges the reality of not taking data or findings as simple and accurate accounts of social phenomena, but representations that are as near to the real events as the activity of research and textual reconstructions of its outcomes, will allow.

Selecting the Methods

The justification for the chosen methodological techniques (described in detail below) is one of pragmatism. That is, the methods flow logically from the research questions and the aims of the project. The questions and aims are themselves the logical consequence of the theoretical considerations of the research and the outcomes of the pre-pilot and pilot stages of the research design.

Furthermore, these particular methods were selected because they are efficient. That is, given the inevitable restrictions on time, resources and access to research arenas, they are the most practicable.

In addressing the goals of the research, both inter-methodological and intra-methodological triangulation has been adopted. Inter-methodological triangulation refers to the use of different methods within a research design and intra-methodological triangulation refers to the use of different techniques within each method (for example, open and closed questions in the Diary-interview Schedule; standardised questions and investigative probes in the Focused-interview Schedule).

Consequently, the methodological tools in the study transgress the conventional divide between quantitative and qualitative research methodology. For Bryman (1988), the overlapping of quantitative and qualitative methodologies is not only vindicated for pragmatic reasons. He suggests that the epistemological bifurcation of research in this way is based on a false premise. Bryman provides examples of ethnographic studies which at various levels operated with some of the principles associated with positivism. For example, he suggests that ethnographers are committed, either tacitly or manifestly, to empiricism. Bryman demonstrates also that many quantitative researchers attempt to discover 'meaning' (or *'verstehen'*) behind social action, which is seen usually to be a principle of qualitative research.

Methodology

Ten CPNs, operating in four different teams in the North of England, were studied sequentially over a two-year period. Approximately 25 new referrals were monitored from each CPN (252 in total).

About 18 months before the study began, I was seconded from Teesside Polytechnic (now the University of Teesside), where I was employed as a lecturer, to work part-time as a CPN in a CMHT for one year (the equivalent of six months full-time). This provided me with the experience of community psychiatric nursing that would enable me to lead post-registration courses for psychiatric nurses working in the community. The English National Board for Nursing, Health Visiting and Midwifery, requires a minimum period of six months working as a CPN (along with other criteria) before a lecturer can become a leader of a post-basic community psychiatric nursing course.

However, this experience also allowed me to assess more specifically the concerns of CPNs with regard to their participation in CMHTs and to formalise the research design for this study. These concerns had been expressed during earlier exploratory discussions between myself and CPNs from a variety of health authorities.

The CPNs expected involvement in the CMHTs to alter the relationship between themselves and members of other disciplines (particularly psychiatry). The consequence of belonging to a CMHT, the CPNs argued, re-established a previous hierarchical structure that existed in the psychiatric hospitals whereby the consultant psychiatrist was dominant in his or (less frequently) her professional relationship with the nursing staff. For the CPNs, therefore, membership would undermine the clinical independence they purported to experience. For example, the CPNs and their managers in the health authority in which I worked had challenged the position of dominance by the psychiatrists over nurses through the adoption of an open referral system (i.e. accepting clients from any source rather than just from the psychiatrist). However, confirming what other CPNs had explained to me, the psychiatrists (and some members of the other mental health disciplines) in this health authority were indicating that they were discontented with these arrangements. It was this area of inter-occupational strife that became the focus for the study reported here.

The pre-pilot experience also helped in my acclimatisation to the cultural, behavioural and linguistic norms of community psychiatric nursing. It therefore increased my understanding of the CPN's occupational role and social function. That is, it helped me to avoid 'communicative blunders' (Briggs, 1986) in the collection and analysis of data that involved human subjects as the primary source of information.

The pilot study was conducted in a health authority that was not included in the main part of the project. The objective of the pilot study was to judge the feasibility of implementing the chosen research procedures and to ensure that these procedures were germane to the aims of the study.

Although the review of the pilot study demonstrated that the overall research strategy was appropriate in meeting the aims of the research, minor changes to the selected procedures were put into place. However, with reference to the 'quality' of the data, one alteration was of significance. Much more time would have to be made available for the interviews than I had previously intended. I had calculated, before the piloting of the methods, that I would ask for no more than about half an hour per week from each of the CPNs for regular interviewing about their work and about 45 minutes for the other interviews. Moreover, I had made a particular point of (informally) contracting with the participants that I would take the minimum time possible to collect data so as not to be too intrusive on their normal routines. The time actually taken in the interview was considerably longer. None of the interviewees, however, complained about this. Conversely, they appeared to welcome the opportunity to talk about what was going on in their everyday working lives.

The Diary

A Diary-interview Schedule (Appendix 1) formed the core research tool for examining the clinical autonomy and levels of negotiation exercised by the 10 psychiatric nurses. The CMHTs were studied in turn over two years, with the action reportedly taken by the CPNs on 252 new referrals (made to them directly or via the CMHT) being monitored. The Diary-interview Schedule provided a detailed account of the relevant aspects of the CPN's professional practice and her or his interpretation of that practice, from which quantitative as well as qualitative data were extrapolated.

On a weekly basis, each CPN from the CMHT being studied at the time, was interviewed. Studies by Zimmerman and Wieder (1977), Parnell (1978) and Burgess (1983) are examples of diaries being used where the informants enter the data. However, rather than the informant entering information in the Diary-interview Schedule, I recorded the data during the interview, or (using a tape recording of the session to maintain accuracy) later the same day.

The Diary-interview format reduced the problem of non-compliance and allowed the data to be checked for internal validity. It also offered the opportunity for the immediate probing of incidental data. The probing style in this research is an adaptation of two probing schemes. Zimmerman and Wieder (1977) provide the first schema with their general 'who', 'what', 'when', 'where' and 'how' questioning formula:

> 'The "What?" involved a description of the activity or discussion recorded in the diarist's own categories. "When?" involved reference to the time and timing of the activity, with special attention to recording the actual sequence of events. "Where?" involved a designation of the location of the activity ... The "How?" involved a description of whatever logistics were entailed by the activity' (p486).

The second schema is offered by Adams and Schvaneveldt (1985) and contains six categories: 'The *completion* probe is an invitation to expand ... *clarification* ... [is] primarily concerned with explaining something in more detail ... [the] *channel* probe is used to determine the origin ... of a comment ... *hypothetical* probes are useful ... to understand alternatives or variations of attitude ... *reactive* probes are designed to bring out additional affective reactions or feelings ... *high pressure* [probes] ... to ... push a respondent to the ultimate truth as he or she sees it' [emphasis by Adams and Schvaneveldt] (p224).

The structure and content of the Diary-interview Schedule (the type of questions, the phrasing of the questions and the order in which they appeared) was pre-formulated, standardised and pre-coded after the pilot study. However, the questioning remained flexible by taking into account the individual concerns of the CPNs, incidental and unexpected happenings that required probing and the element of evolutionary change to the agenda. Therefore, the Diary-interview Schedule took on the character of a longitudinal in-depth interview. That is, the meaning of the CPN's actions was investigated through a number of closed questions, open questions (some of which were retrospectively coded and categorised) and a rolling programme of innovative questions – all of which occurred over a prolonged period of time.

All sessions were tape recorded in their entirety. Tape recording the sessions with the CPNs allowed for the material disclosed to be analysed later. It provided the security that no data would be forgotten or missed and it offered the opportunity to clarify notes made during the interview. What was not usually recorded on tape were the backstage and hidden-agenda discussions to which I had access.

The Diary-interview Schedule contains three distinct sections. The first section records personal and professional information about the CPN. This was completed in a preliminary interview with the CPN following at least one visit to the centre to talk to the CPNs collectively. During this first visit, the CPNs were briefed about my research. In the case of one CMHT, all the team members were present for this briefing. When completing this first section of the Diary-Interview Schedule, I concentrated on building a relationship and on allaying any anxieties concerning the research (for example, about managers being able to identify exactly who the informants were).

In the second section of the Diary-interview Schedule, data were recorded about the referral pathways of the clients monitored in the study. The first part of this section contains specific details relating to the source of the referrals and the social and medical background of the clients. The reasons why the CPN had accepted the clients on to her or his case load were also recorded here. The question relating to the expectations of the person who referred the client to the CPN was compiled from Barratt (1989). The list of possible situations for CPNs to conduct their sessions with clients has been taken from Parnell (1978).

What action the CPNs had taken, with respect to the treatment and management of the clients, was recorded in the third section of the schedule. A series of probes are listed at the start of this section, based on Zimmerman and Wieder's (1977) and Adams and Schvaneveldt's (1985) formulae. This inventory served as an *aide-mémoire* and checklist during the interviews.

Specific data were collected relating to any direct contact that had occurred in the week preceding the interview between the CPN and the client (for example, how much time had been spent with the client and the content of the interaction). Details were also entered in the third section concerning any discussions that had taken place between the

CPN and, for example, other members of the CMHT or the general practitioner.

Focused-interviewing

In-depth interviewing was used as the specific tool for the retrieval of data from the CPNs' colleagues on the CMHT and their managers (as well as being used to complete the Diary-interview Schedule). The type of interview employed to gain data from the CPNs' colleagues and managers can be described as semi-structured or 'focused'.

A number of themes relating directly to the aims of the research were prepared before the interview and indicative questions were written in the Focused-interview Schedule (Appendix 2). However, the manner in which specific questions were delivered in the interview and the order in which they appeared, varied according to the style and content of the interaction. The interviews of the CPNs' colleagues and managers, therefore, had a framework that consisted of topics I wished to explore. However, other relevant areas not contained explicitly in the schedule, but which surfaced during the interview, were also probed. Thus, as with the Diary-interview Schedule, the Focused-interview Schedule's pre-formulated categories became (at least in part) catalysts for producing some respondent-centred data.

Furthermore, the dynamic disposition of the methodology in this project came into play with respect to the content of the Focused-interviews. Topics that were either specific to the interviewee, or the CMHT in question, were fed into the interview. Issues that were referred to in the Focused-interviews were adopted, where appropriate, for subsequent interviews (either with the CPNs or other members of the CMHT). A number of amendments were made to the Focused-interview Schedule when issues were constantly being raised by the interviewee, but which had not been included in the original schedules.

Six consultant psychiatrists and five social workers (including those from the pilot study), three psychologists (one of whom represented psychology in two of the CMHTs), four occupational therapists and four nurse managers, were interviewed. Most of the interviews were about an hour long, although two lasted nearly one and a half hours each. They were conducted in a room at the informant's place of work, with only myself and the informant present. These interviews took place generally between the middle and the end of the period spent eliciting data from the CPNs at the team centre in question. However, occasionally, because of holidays or difficulties in arranging appointments (one consultant psychiatrist cancelled two meetings), the interviews were carried out after I had completed the collection of data from the CPNs in that particular CMHT.

As with the Diary-interviews, the Focused-interviews were tape recorded. However, one consultant psychiatrist and two occupational therapists refused to be taped. The consultant who refused to be tape recorded explained that he was afraid that his remarks might be taken 'out of context'. He made reference to the now deceased Lord Denning, who was in dispute with a journalist from the also extinct *Spectator* newspaper about 'off the record' material that had been tape recorded and printed against Denning's wishes. The dispute had surfaced in the media on the previous day to my interview with the consultant. The two occupational therapists who did not want to be tape recorded were from different teams, but the same centre. They both stated, independently of each other, that they were 'nervous in front of a microphone'. For these three unrecorded interviews, notes were made during the interview, verbal notes made immediately after the interview and then a full set of notes compiled either that day or the next day.

Following all of the other interviews, verbal notes were tape recorded and then transcribed along with the content of the interview. When appropriate, written comments were added to the relevant section of the Field-notebook. For example, this occurred when amendments to the interview schedule were required, or if I needed to clarify an issue with the CPNs that had been raised by their colleagues in the Focused-interview sessions.

An attempt was made at the beginning of the interview to relax the informant and to engender trust. The specific strategies used to accomplish this varied depending on the informant's social role, whether or not she or he was already known to me (for example, because she or he had attended an educational programme at Teesside Polytechnic) and how much time she or he stated could be given to the interview on that particular day. In the main, my approach consisted of conversational 'small-talk', as well as an imprecise description of the aims of the research. My introduction was deliberately vague – I stated that I was 'interested in the role of the CPN in the CMHT' – in order to invite responses to my subsequent questions that were as uncontaminated as possible by the informant being too focused on the precise aims of the study. Furthermore, the initial scene-setting involved my selecting a role title from a number of possibilities. Taking cognisance of Freidson's observation that medical practitioners were more forthcoming with patients with whom they believed they had a 'cultural affinity' (Freidson, 1988, p321), I stated I was a 'researcher' to all of the informants, except the CPN managers. With regard to the latter group, most of the managers perceived me as a 'lecturer from the Poly'.

The final version of the Focused-interview Schedule contains five categories of questions. Although the questions are grouped, the sequence of the questioning and concomitant probing followed the natural flow of the interview.

The first category invited the informants to comment on what they understood the role of the CPN to be. Next, the informants were asked for their views on the CPN's clinical function with the client, particularly in relation to how much autonomy the CPN should have with regard to accepting or refusing referrals, assessment, making decisions about treatment and discharging clients.

Questions in the third and fourth categories elicited opinions from the informant about the type of management, supervisory and organisational structures she or he believed the CPN should belong to. The last category contained questions that asked the interviewee to describe a 'good' and 'bad' CPN as ideal types, as well as what could be put into place to improve CPN practice. At the end of the interview, the informants were asked to add any comments that they hadn't made already, but felt were relevant to the topics under discussion.

Field Observations

Apart from the two main research methodologies (i.e. the Diary-interviews and the Focused-interviews), more than 150 hours of observation took place during the study. Extended periods of time were spent sitting in the team office or a central area within the team centre. The periods of observation took place following each set of interviews with the CPNs and after the interviewing of their colleagues and managers.

Observations made were entered into a Field-notebook (Appendix 3). Following Burgess (1981), the entries consisted of observations of substantive events, preconceptual interpretations of these events and the data from the interviews and comments on methodological issues. Substantive observations had, at the outset of the data collecting period, been perceived as fulfilling the secondary purpose of complementing and triangulating the data obtained from the other two methods.

However, unique substantive areas emerged from these observations. Many of these areas were explored further during subsequent interviews with the CPNs, their colleagues or their managers. My reflections about what I had observed contributed also to the refining of the questions in the Diary-interview Schedule and Focused-interview Schedule.

The practical side of recording the data involved the writing of key descriptive words and short statements in the notebook as events were occurring (but only if this did not become distracting or intimidating for the people under observation). In the early stages of collecting data, a full description of the observed significant events, methodological comments, etc., was written in the notebook later the same day. Eventually, however, what I found more effective (as with the interviews) was to tape record my observations as soon as I had left the relevant centre. This meant that what I had seen and heard could be reported at the earliest possible moment. The information recorded in this way had the advantage of being fresh and relatively undistorted from its original form.

Role and Rapport

My role was, at times, that of 'non-participant' because I would be observing without my presence being acknowledged actively. At other times, I was more participatory because I would be included in the discussions held between, for example, the CPNs or between the CPNs and other team members.

Involvement in these discussions occurred both within the working environment and, occasionally, at social events which I had been invited to attend by the CPNs. In this latter role I seemed to be viewed as an interested and familiar visitor who, although not essentially part of the CMHT, was nevertheless seen to be associated with the CPN section of the team. This association was most noticeable when the research was coming to the end in the respective health authorities. For example, I found it difficult to close my involvement with a team as I realised that I would be losing contact with people I had gained some degree of personal attachment to and some of the CPNs openly expressed their (apparently genuine) sorrow at my eventual departure. This element of what an anthropologist might describe as 'going native' was probably because I have a background in psychiatric nursing and have worked as a CPN.

When my role as observer was nearer 'participant' than 'non-participant', it resulted in much more data being supplied by the CPNs about how they operated with their clients than I believe would have been forthcoming otherwise. When this role was combined with other techniques aimed at increasing the informality of the relationship between the researcher and the respondent during an interview (such as avoiding directing my attention to the physical entity of the Diary-Interview Schedule), then the content and style of the interchanges became much more fluid.

The development of an effective rapport with the informant is made all the more possible if the communication skills of 'active listening' and 'empathy' are employed by the researcher. When a researcher is attempting to obtain qualitative data, the skill of listening serves a complex series of functions. It involves not just 'attending' (i.e. demonstrating to the informant through one's non-verbal behaviour that she or he is being 'listened to'), but engaging in a dialogue with the other person. That is, there is a need not only to use eye contact, posture, etc., but also to participate in the conversation.

Backstage

The development of an effective rapport with the CPNs, however, produced the major ethical dilemma of the research. Using skills such as active listening and empathy stimulated the CPNs and their colleagues into producing in-depth responses to the questions I posed. But the more carefully and empathetically I listened, the more I was given access to information that Goffman (1959, p114) has described as 'back-region' or 'backstage' conversations. The access to this type of data caused me some concern during the study, as I was to register in the Field-notes: 'Am I getting too familiar with the CPNs? This may help me to uncover more material as they trust me, but they would not want me to if they thought I might record it.'

For example, when team members congregated in a communal office I was privy to what appeared to be customary and unguarded interchanges between the CPNs and between the CPNs and their colleagues. I was also often accepted as a 'confidant' in the research interviews. This had the consequence of the CPNs (and sometimes their colleagues) providing me with intimate details about the other team members, managers and the organisation to which they belonged. Moreover, I was occasionally allowed to observe, and even partake in, practices that could be deemed unprofessional.

These backstage accounts and observations were, however, invaluable in contextualising and validating data obtained through the interviews. The compromise I have reached over this material is to regard the CPNs as having accepted implicitly that I was researching throughout the time I was in contact with them and, therefore, only if I was asked specifically not to report on a particular event, would I deliberately ignore data. Where I have used information supplied in this way (i.e. in the 'results' section below) it is unattributed.

However, this does not resolve completely the ethical dilemma with regard to having access to backstage data. It could be argued that when the subjects of a study agree to allow themselves to be observed or interviewed in-depth, they are doing so without knowing the rules of the game. That is, they would be unaware of exactly what might be observed and recorded, or how events might be packaged and interpreted.

Reactivity

When a participatory role in research is adopted, it is usual to regard the effect that the researcher is having on those that are being observed or interviewed as a disadvantage. These effects may be so insidious that they are not noticeable to either the researcher or her or his subjects.

The tape recording of the interviews, however, enabled me to appraise the effects of reactivity to some degree. For example, following an interview, I would listen to the tape and ensure leading, biased, value-laden, ambiguous or unclear questioning was not repeated in the next interview. Where reactivity had occurred and was not eradicated at the time, attempts have been made to account for this when the data were analysed.

On occasions in this research, my presence had not a small and hidden effect, but a major and very noticeable one. It was, for example, to alter radically the clinical practice of the CPN, the psychiatric career of a client or the size of the CPN's case load: 'The CPN commented upon something I had already realised was going on. He said that when I asked him questions I "jogged" his memory and prompted him to do things that he had otherwise forgotten to do (for example, contacting people he should have liaised with; discharging clients he should have discharged earlier)' (Field-notes).

When I was interviewing another CPN (and this was not the first time that this had happened with this particular CPN) I asked: 'So you're thinking of discharging her [the client]?' The CPN replied: 'I've just thought about it now. She's discharged! What would I do without you keeping me numbers down!'

The act of asking questions about what the CPNs had been doing with their clients, and inadvertently offering the CPNs an opportunity to reflect on their practice, resulted in action that otherwise might not have occurred (or at least would not have happened until a later date).

Rather than viewing this as a methodological problem, however, the very fact that my presence served as an *aide-mémoire* and a stimulus for a change in procedure, provided a further source of data that had direct relevance to the aims of the study. The CPN, reacting to a researcher's questions in this way, displayed 'clinical fallibility' (by forgetting to carry out certain actions that she or he regarded as necessary). Where 'mistakes' in practice can be corrected without recourse to discussions with colleagues, supervisors or managers, then this indicates that the CPNs in these circumstances enjoy a high degree of freedom in their actions.

Validity

To have internal validity, a research design must demonstrate that it observes or measures what it intends to measure, rival causes or alternative hypotheses are discounted and spurious conclusions avoided. That is, the results must be representative of what happened in the research.

The most obvious form of internal validity is that of 'face validity'. Face validity is when the proposed research is subjected to peer and 'expert' scrutiny and opinions are sought about the fit between the aims of the research and its methodological procedures. The design of this study was shown to a number of CPNs and academic colleagues and their views were taken into consideration.

Achieving internal validity is of particular importance in experimental research. However, attempts have been made in this study to deal with a number of the extraneous variables that weaken this form of validity (Cook and Campbell, 1979). For example, the effect of my presence in the research situation (as I have already commented above) was to some extent monitored by the CPNs themselves declaring the influence I was having on their practice. Furthermore, the effect of 'maturation' (i.e. the changes that occur in people and organisations over a period of time) can be measured in this study. That is, the early tape recordings of the interviews can be compared with the later ones.

The teams were chosen on the basis of their geographical accessibility. To reduce researcher bias in the process of selecting the teams, the nurse managers in the health authorities used in the study were asked to nominate the CMHTs. However, this procedure may have produced bias from the managers, although none was detected in the analysis of the data.

Internal validity is enhanced substantially through the use of methodological and data triangulation (Denzin, 1970). Methodological triangulation was secured both 'within method' (one research tool was used consistently on many different occasions with the same subjects) and 'between method'. Data triangulation was obtained through the study of the CPNs over a fairly long time, the collection of data at various levels (i.e. individual and group) and through the comparison of the four CMHTs.

External validity refers to the ability of the concepts and theories propagated by the research to be applied generally. As this research project is a case study, there is no intention to generalise from the specific in any positivistic sense. The sample used is not described as representative of all CPNs or CMHTs. However, qualified observations, which may have broader implications, are made with regard to community psychiatric nursing and the care of the mentally ill. This, I believe, is legitimate on the basis that case study research can provide useful insights that can inform policy decisions and stimulate debate, as well as lead to further research.

Furthermore, this project is a multiple case study in that a number of CMHTs were studied. This provides comparative data, which does not compensate for the selection and sampling requirements necessary for statistical generalisations, but has some merit in terms of what can be deduced about the workings of other CMHTs.

The potential generalisability of these insights, however, is also dependent on content, construct and ecological validity of the study.

Content validity examines the representativeness of the items measuring the construct being studied. In this project, I followed the 'brainstorming' and 'best fit' procedure, as described by Kane (1984), when selecting and grouping items for inclusion in the Diary-interview Schedule and the Focused-interview Schedule. Individual test items have also been collected through the extraction of key concepts from the review of the germane literature on 'professionalism' and 'mental health nursing'.

Construct validity deals with the question of how well are the underlying theoretical constructs being measured. There are two elements to construct validity, convergent validity and discriminant validity (Kidder, 1981). Convergent validity has been achieved by gaining information on CPN practice from the CPNs themselves and by comparing their accounts with those of their colleagues and managers, as well as with my own observations. The achievement of discriminant validity has been made possible through the inclusion of appropriately discriminating questions in the schedules (e.g. relating to perceptions of autonomy in the professional practice of non-CPNs and ideal role-performance criteria for CPNs).

Ecological validity raises the question of what is the match between the everyday world of the people being researched and the techniques employed by the researcher. The longitudinal nature of the interviewing I conducted with the CPNs, and the cultural compatibility I had with them, gives a high level of ecological validity. The ecological validity of the Focused-interviews (with the CPNs' colleagues and managers), however, did not achieve the same standard. These interviews were one-off sessions, which meant that there was less time to connect the intricacies of the everyday world of these informants to that of the research process.

Reliability

Internal reliability is achieved if other researchers find that constructs produced from data in a previous research project coincide with their own constructions. External validity is closely linked with internal reliability.

Strategies adopted by this researcher to increase internal reliability include a description of the analytical process used to refine the data (see below). Moreover, the full interview transcriptions and field notes are available (Morrall, 1995a) to allow public inspection of the logic of the inferences being made.

Furthermore, two colleagues, both of whom have a background in research and in community psychiatric nursing, were asked to peruse the original qualitative data and the subsequent conceptual extractions. Their comments were used to help modify the final theoretical conclusions.

If independent researchers (operating in similar situations) produce the same constructs and conclusions as previous researchers, then the first research design can be said to have external reliability. This can be extraordinarily difficult to accomplish in any research project, even those that are experimental in design. However, LeCompte and Goetz (1982) suggest a number of ways in which external reliability may be attempted. For example, they recommend that the researcher states clearly the role (or roles) that she or he enacts in the research situation. The underlying premises, units of analysis and methods of data collection and analysis also need to be delineated. These strategies (which have been introduced into this study) enable any future researcher to identify the nuances of the project she or he wishes to replicate.

LeCompte and Goetz (1982) suggest also that the characteristics of the informants and the social settings in which the data are collected should be described in detail. Unfortunately, such details would jeopardise the commitment I have made to all of the participants in the research to maintain anonymity and, therefore, I have been circumspect in my descriptions of the personal attributes of the participants and their social settings.

Retesting of the methods and comparing results has occurred in this project as the four case studies were researched consecutively. However, this was not an independent test of reliability as I was the sole researcher involved in all the cases. Furthermore, I have made an argument for the vigorous and deliberate inclusion of methodological reflexivity in this project and this undermines considerably the external reliability of the study. That is, altering the research design while data are being collected (in order to increase internal validity) has the effect of decreasing external reliability.

Analysis

Following the collection of the data from the interviews and the observations, the tape recordings of the CPN interviews were considered first. Data relevant to the aims of the research were transcribed from the tape recordings of these interviews. The tape recordings of the interviews with the CPNs were also used to help check the accuracy of the data entered in the Diary-interview Schedules at the time of the interviews and to complete any missing factors. Data relating to the open questions in the Diary-interview Schedule (Questions 72 and 93: Appendix 1) were extracted from these tape recordings and categories produced and coded retrospectively. Although Question 76, which refers to the therapeutic style used by the CPN when she or he was with a client, had categories that were organised prior to the interviewing of the CPNs, it was delivered as an open question ('What did you do with the client?'). Therefore, qualitative data from the tape recordings addressing this question were also collated.

The quantitative data from the Diary-Interview Schedule were then subjected to statistical analysis using the PC Microsoft Windows version of the Statistical Package for the Social Sciences. Initially, descriptive statistics (e.g. frequencies; means; modes; medians; cross-tabulations) of all of the pre-coded and post-coded quantifiable data were produced. These were reviewed and selected variables were then measured for levels of association. Specifically, the selected variables were analysed using Chi-square and non-parametric correlation testing (e.g. Cramer's V; Phi Coefficient; Kruskal-Wallis; Spearman's RHO).

The tape recordings of the interviews with the CPNs' colleagues and managers were transcribed verbatim. All of the transcriptions (together with the notes taken from those interviews that were not tape recorded) and the substantive and pre-analytical Field-notes, were analysed. The procedure (adapted from Burnard, 1991) for analysing the qualitative data from the Diary-Interview Schedules, the Focused-Interview Schedules and the substantive and pre-analytical Field-notes, involved the following stages:

1. Immediately after the CPN interviews and focused interviews took place, comments on the content of the interview were entered in the Field-notebook.
2. At the end of the data collecting period, all the tape recordings of the interviews were listened to and the notes from the interviews that were not tape recorded were read, without any comments being written.
3. The tapes of the CPN interviews were then listened to again and a number of headings produced: data supporting these headings were transcribed, coded and classified.
4. All the interviews of the CPNs' colleagues and managers were transcribed: these were read and re-read and then the data were coded and classified under headings.
5. The substantive and analytical Field-notes were read and re-read and data coded and classified under headings.
6. The headings from the CPN interviews, focused interviews and the Field-notes were compared with the pre-organised headings. A composite list of headings was then collated from these two sources.

Summary

In this chapter I have outlined the plan of my own research study in which I investigated particular spheres of psychiatric nursing work relating to professionalism. The design of the study is offered in detail so that the reader can judge the merits and deficits of my interpretation and presentation of the results, discussion, inferences and recommendations contained in the remaining parts of the book.

Chapter 6
Case Study:
Results

The results of the study I am using to explore the issue of profession-alism and mental health nursing are presented and evaluated in this chapter. First, background information is supplied about the CPNs who participated in the study and the 252 referrals that were monitored. The remaining subsections relate to the aims of the research (in partic-ular, the degree of clinical autonomy experienced by the CPNs).

Specifically, the following issues are examined: the referrer's expec-tations and the reasons given by the CPN for accepting a referral; the amount of discussion that was reported to take place between the CPN and her or his colleagues, supervisor and manager; the procedures used by the CPNs to discharge a client, or gain in-patient care for a client; the reported content of the CPN's direct involvement with her or his clients; what membership of the CMHT means for the CPN; super-vision, conflict and hierarchy in the team; the methods used by the CPN to undermine the 'dominance' of her or his practice by others in the team; the role of the CPN, as perceived by her or his manager and col-leagues.

The CPNs

Six of the CPNs in the study were male and four female. Four of the CPNs were aged between 20 and 29 years, three between 30 and 39 years and three between 40 and 49 years. All of the CPNs were regis-tered mental nurses, with three also being registered general nurses. Only two had a community psychiatric nursing qualification, although two others were undertaking a course to gain this qualification at the time of the study. One CPN had a counselling qualification, another a diploma in psychotherapy and a third had the Diploma in Nursing.

Four of the CPNs had gained their basic mental nurse qualification before 1980, four between 1980 and 1985 and two after 1986. Three had been trained under the '1982' syllabus (ENB/WNB, 1982). The pre-

76

vious syllabus emphasised medical approaches to the treatment of the mentally ill, whereas the 1982 syllabus pointed to the importance of including social factors, interpersonal skills, counselling, personal development and aspects of 'new nursing' in the training and education of mental health nurses.

A core element of the new nursing introduced in the 1982 syllabus was the 'nursing process'. This encourages nurses to formulate specific plans for the treatment of each client. However, as I discuss below, there is little evidence of the nursing process being implemented by the CPNs in this study. Nor do the data indicate that the majority of CPNs have moved significantly from the influence of medical interpretations of mental distress.

Seven of the CPNs had spent more than one year working in the community (with three of the seven having spent at least five years) and three less than one year. Nine of the CPNs were employed at the level of charge nurse (either grade F or G). The one exception was employed as a staff nurse (grade E).

The managers of the CPNs reported that some differentiation in role function existed between the grades. For example, charge nurses were expected to supervise the clinical work of staff nurses and staff nurses were not supposed to do the initial assessment of new clients. However, the CPNs reported (and their assertions are supported by the data from the study) that there was very little difference in how the various grades operated in reality.

The size of the CPNs' case loads ranged from between 10 and 20 clients (for three CPNs), to more than 41 (for two of the CPNs). The remaining five CPNs had case loads of between 21 and 40 clients. However, what constituted a 'case load' was not consistent or obvious. For example, one of the CPNs explained that she had three categories of clients within what she classified as her case load. These were: (i) clients receiving visits on a regular basis; (ii) clients on the health authority's computerised 'monitor' system, which would send automatically a reminder to make contact with certain vulnerable clients who were not formally part of the CPN's case load; (iii) a number of 'inactive' clients who might be re-referred at some time in the future.

The Referrals

The measurement of the CPNs' levels of clinical autonomy is centred on the forms of action that were taken with the 252 new clients received over the two years during which data were collected. The amount of time the clients were monitored in the research was dependent on whether or not they were discharged (or re-referred) before the end of a maximum period of three months. Fifty-three (21%) of the referrals in the study were monitored for 11 weeks or more and 71 (28.2%) between five and 10 weeks. The remainder were reviewed for periods of between one week and four weeks (Table 1).

The direct referral source for 38.9% (n = 98) of the clients was a general practitioner, with 22.6% (n = 57) being referred by the consultant psychiatrist or a member of her or his medical team (Table 2). Forty-one (16.3%) of the clients were referred by other agencies. This included the staff of local authority residential homes, senior nurses from psychiatric hospital wards where the client was an in-patient, or relatives and neighbours of the client.

Self-referrals accounted for 19 (7.5%) of the clients. However, only 0.8% (n = 2) of the clients were stated by the CPNs to have been referred by the CMHT as a collective entity. A high proportion (76.6%; n = 193) of clients were referred directly to the CPNs. That is, there was only a small number of clients being passed from one referrer to another before reaching the CPN.

The gender division of the clients was: 61.5% (n = 155) female; and 38.5% (n = 97) male. Nearly a third (32.9%; n = 83) of the clients were single, with 42.5% (n = 107) married and 17% (n = 43) separated or divorced. The age of the clients spread from less than 20 years (3.2%; n = 8) to over 60 years (13.5%; n = 34). Sixty-four (25.4%) were between the ages of 20 and 29 years and 51 (20.2%) between 30 and 39 years. Forty-eight (19%) were between 40 and 49 years and forty-seven (18.7%) between 50 and 59.

The majority of the clients were not in paid employment, with 36.5% (n = 92) unemployed, 19.8% (n = 50) housewives (with one house-husband), 14.7% (n = 37) retired and 1.2% (n = 3) full-time students.

Of those clients in paid employment, none were in the Registrar General's socio-economic group A (professional/managerial). Ten (4.0%) of the clients were in group B (semi-professional/supervisory), 12 (4.8%) in group C (skilled manual and non-manual), 20 (7.9%) in group D (semi-skilled) and 11 (4.4%) in group E (unskilled). A further 17 (6.7%) were in part-time paid employment (semi-skilled or unskilled).

Only 21.4% (n = 54) of the clients had no previous involvement with a general practitioner or the psychiatric services with respect to their mental health. This contact with the formal psychiatric services included hospitalisation, out-patient treatment and/or having been a former client of a CPN. In-patient psychiatric treatment had been experienced by 44.4% (n = 112) of the clients.

The CPNs were asked during the Diary-interviews to state what they considered to be the major problem with each of the new referrals (Table 3). Sixty-four (25.4%) were described as suffering from depression and 49 (19.4%) from anxiety. Delusions and/or hallucinations were seen by the CPN to be the paramount problem in 16.7% (n = 42) of the cases. Reasons that either explicitly or implicitly were given as 'problems with living' accounted for 11.5% (n = 29) of the referrals. A further 7.9% (n = 20) were unclassified because the CPN could not identify any problem at all, or one issue in particular. Most of these latter clients did, however, remain on the CPNs' case loads.

At the end of the research, 56% (n = 141) of the clients remained under the care of the CPN who had first accepted them. Twenty-nine (11.5%) of the clients were re-referred to another practitioner specifically for the continuation of mental health care. The majority of these re-referrals were sent to health care professionals who did not belong to the CMHT. Eighty-one (32.1%) of the clients were discharged during the research.

Table 1: Length of Time the Referrals were Monitored (Q.70 of the Diary-interview Schedule)

Value label	Value	Frequency	Percent	Cum. percent
One week only	1	46	18.3	18.3
Two to four weeks	2	82	32.5	50.8
Five to seven weeks	3	45	17.9	68.7
Eight to ten weeks	4	26	10.3	79.0
Eleven or more weeks	5	53	21.0	100.0
Total		252	100.0	

Table 2: Immediate Source of the Referrals (Q.55 of the Diary-interview Schedule)

Value label	Value	Frequency	Percent	Cum. percent
Consultant psychiatrist	1	40	15.9	15.9
Other psychiatrist	2	17	6.7	22.6
General practitioner	3	98	38.9	61.5
MPOTA	4	2	.8	62.3
Social worker	5	3	1.2	63.5
Psychologist	6	3	1.2	64.7
CPN	7	16	6.3	71.0
CMHT	10	2	.8	71.8
Health visitor	12	6	2.4	74.2
Manager	15	5	2.0	76.2
Self-referred	16	19	7.5	83.7
Other	18	41	16.3	100.0
Total		252	100.0	

Key:
Other psychiatrist – other member of psychiatric medical team
MPOTA – medical practitioner other than above

Table 3: The CPN's View of the Client's Mental Health Problem (Q.68 of the Diary-interview Schedule)

Value label	Value	Frequency	Percent	Cum. percent
Anxiety	1	49	19.4	19.4
Depression	2	64	25.4	44.8
Phobia	3	7	2.8	47.6
Delusions	4	7	2.8	50.4
Delusions and hallucinations	6	35	13.9	64.3
Confusion	7	2	.8	65.1
Overactivity	8	8	3.2	68.3
Aggression	9	5	2.0	70.2
Self-harm (actual)	10	4	1.6	71.8
Self-harm (implied)	11	4	1.6	73.4
Drug/alcohol addiction	12	12	4.8	78.2
Problems with living	13	29	11.5	89.7
Sexual problems	14	4	1.6	91.3
Eating problems	15	2	.8	92.1
Other	16	20	7.9	100.00
Total		252	100.0	

Expectations

The CPNs were asked in the Diary-interviews if the person referring the client had stated what form of treatment (or any other action) she or he wanted to be carried out. This question was aimed in part at establishing how the referrer perceived the CPN. That is, if the CPN is asked to undertake a specific task then this may suggest that the person making the request views the CPN as someone in a subordinate position to herself or himself. Contrarily, if the referrer does not ask for a named therapeutic intervention to be executed, then this may imply that she or he believes the CPN to be an independent practitioner who is capable of reviewing effectively the client's condition and deciding on the correct approach to take without any guidance. Of course, these accounts of what the referrer expected were open to 'reinterpretation' by the CPN. However, on many occasions, corroborative evidence was available in the form of written communications from the referrer.

More fundamental to the evaluation of the CPN's level of clinical autonomy is the reaction of the CPN to the requests from the referrer and whether or not these expectations were consummated. The expectations of the referrer serve as a base-line from which the CPN can decide (or not decide) to act autonomously.

For example, if CPNs perceive themselves as merely providers of technical services (i.e. as skilled workers rather than fully-fledged professionals), then the request would be accepted without marked disapprobation. On the other hand, if CPNs view themselves to be autonomous practitioners, then they may be antagonistic towards the people making such demands. If CPNs are autonomous in reality, then they may reject the suggestions made by the referrers.

I was interested also in what kind of tasks the referrers were asking the CPNs to complete. That is, were they predominantly routine, menial and low-status assignments, or relatively prestigious and elaborate? For example, assessing a client's mental state should be regarded as complex and high-status work. The consequence for the client of entering into the psychiatric system can be quite detrimental to her or his future prospects, particularly with regard to employment. If a client is not offered help from the psychiatric services when this is needed, the effect could be even more dramatic, as has been witnessed in the cases of Christopher Clunis who committed homicide after a 'catalogue of failure and missed opportunity' (Ritchie, 1994, p105) by the psychiatric services and Jason Mitchell who killed three people after being discharged into the community (Blom-Cooper et al., 1996).

However, in this study, the task of assessing the client's mental state was explicitly requested by the referrer for only 17.5% (n = 44) of the referrals (Table 4). The two most frequent referrers, the general practitioner and the consultant psychiatrist, differed in the regularity of their requests for assessment. The consultant psychiatrists asked the CPNs to assess five of their 40 referrals (12.5%), whereas from the 98 referrals made by general practitioners, assessment was requested for 25 (25.5%).

But the issue of assessment is not a straightforward one. For example, the CPNs stated that they made their first (and sometimes more than the first) direct contact with a client with the specific purpose of assessing her or him. However, later in this chapter I shall be showing that the CPNs did not appear to carry out assessment procedures as often as they suggested they did. Furthermore, some of the consultant psychiatrists believed it was their ability to perform psychiatric assessments that differentiated their role from that of the CPNs. That is, 'assessment' was used by the psychiatrists as a criterion to justify their status as professionals.

It would appear that when the task of assessing a client was requested, it was commonly in the belief that the CPN would 'take the client off the referrer's hands'. There were, for example, no reported instances of the referrer asking for a detailed account of the assessment. Where one was supplied, this seemed to be the consequence of ritualistic and bureaucratic role-performance by the CPN, rather than a serious attempt to provide a comprehensive explication of the client's mental health for subsequent consideration and comment by the referrer.

The referrers indicated that they wanted the CPN to provide reassurance and/or support for 25 (9.9.%) of the clients and to 'monitor' the client in 14 cases (5.6.%). The monitoring of a client implied that the CPN should report on her or his general mental health and social circumstances, whether or not the client was taking prescribed medication and if there were any side-effects where medication was being used. The consultant psychiatrists requested these relatively low-status tasks for a much higher proportion of their referrals (reassurance/support: 22.5%; monitoring: 12.5%) than did the general practitioners (reassurance: 8.2.%; monitoring: 2%). This could be interpreted as consultant psychiatrists being more willing to place the CPNs in the role of medical adjunct than are general practitioners.

Although the comparatively high-status task of providing a specialist therapy (e.g. de-sensitisation; anxiety management) was requested for just 18 (7.1%) of all of the referrals, the consultant psychiatrists asked the CPNs to undertake this in 10 (25%) of their referrals, whereas the general practitioners requested this for only five (5.1%) of their referrals. If the numbers of requests for the relatively prestigious tasks of assessing a client and providing a specialist therapy are combined with requests for other higher-status forms of involvement (such as counselling and giving the client advice about her or his diagnosis, treatment and prognosis), then the consultant psychiatrists and general practitioners have virtually the same rates (40% for the former and 38.8% for the latter).

Surprisingly, given the emphasis placed on the CPN's role by her or his colleagues as being concerned with medication (during the Focused-interviews), the CPN was asked specifically to supply a client with medication – including the giving of tranquillisers by injection –

Table 4: Expectations of the Referrers (Q.62 of the Diary-interview Schedule: adapted from Barratt, 1989)

Value label	Value	Frequency	Percent	Cum. percent
Assessment	1	44	17.5	17.5
Counselling	2	13	5.2	22.6
Giving medication	3	18	7.1	29.8
Advising	5	4	1.6	31.3
Specialist therapy	7	18	7.1	38.5
Reassurance/support	8	25	9.9	48.4
Monitoring	9	14	5.6	54.0
Evaluating	10	1	.4	54.4
Unspecified	11	102	40.5	94.8
Other	12	13	5.2	100.0
Total		252	100.0	

on only 18 (7.1%) occasions. The majority of these requests (n = 7) came from other referral agencies (mainly from the local authority residential homes). However, some also came from other CPNs (n = 5) because the client was moving away from their area of practice into the catchment area of the CPN to whom the referral was being made.

Most significant of all, however, was that the referrer did not indicate what she or he expected the CPN to do with the client in 40.5% (n = 102) of the 252 new clients in this study. Although social workers and the CMHT as a whole referred only three and two clients respectively, for none of these was the referrer's expectations specified. No details of what the referrer expected of the CPN were given for 12 of the 19 (63.2%) self-referrals, or for three of the six (50%) referrals made by health visitors. Nor were they supplied for 17 of the 41 (41.5%) clients referred by agencies in the classification 'other', two of the five (40%) made by the CPNs' managers, one of the three made by psychologists (33.3%) and five of the 16 (31.3%) made by other CPNs.

Of the 98 referrals made by general practitioners, 46 (46.9%) were referred without any mention of expectations:

Interviewer: 'The GP wasn't specific about what he wanted you to do?'
CPN: 'Never is. Never. I'd reckon nine out of 10 referrals we get are non-directive.'

Unlike the general practitioners, the consultant psychiatrists made their expectations clear in 32 (80%) of their 40 referrals. The reaction of the CPNs to the consultant psychiatrists being more directive than the other referral agents was, in many instances, one of hostility. Their expression of anger was then followed at times by tactics that included various forms of 'skulduggery'.

The significant amount of referrals being made without the referrer stating what she or he wanted the CPN to do may indicate that the CPN was regarded as appropriately skilled to perform the function of assessing the client and to implement treatment programmes. However, the evidence from the interviews with the CPNs' colleagues from the CMHTs would suggest the contrary (see below). Moreover, what seemed to be the implicit and overriding requirement of the CPN was not that a particular form of clinical intervention took place, but that the referrer was relieved of the problem of dealing with the client.

When expectations were specified, the CPNs responded in ways that would suggest much dissonance with regard to their occupational position. That is, the strategies employed to counter instructions from, for example, the consultant psychiatrists, are not those that would be expected from an occupational group that is certain of its status (whether high or low) in the hierarchy of health care professions. Consequently, although the data relating to the expectations of the referrers imply that the CPNs make independent decisions about what type of involvement they will have with clients, this does not infer that they are clinically autonomous. The control by the CPNs over this aspect of the referral process appears in the main to be the result of a lack of clarity by the referrers with regard to what exactly they want from the CPN and/or a lack of insistence that requests are followed through.

Accepting Referrals

The reasons given by the CPNs for deciding to accept the 252 clients on to their case loads are examined in this section (Table 5). The purpose of asking the CPNs why they had agreed to accept a referral is, first, to ascertain whether or not it was the CPNs who independently made the decisions to accept the clients. That is, I wanted to know (as an indicator of clinical autonomy) if the CPNs had control over who they offered their services to. Second, I wanted to know what type of explanations were supplied for accepting the client. For example, was the decision to accept a client based on the objective testing of a client's mental condition, or on a subjective and unstructured assessment. Third, the answers to this question indicate the ways in which the CPNs were able to influence the psychiatric careers of those who had been referred to them.

All but one of the CPNs stated that they had an open referral system. Under this system, the CPN accepts referrals from any source. These sources include consultant psychiatrists, general practitioners, social workers, psychologists, representatives of voluntary organisations, self-referrals and the CMHT as a collective referral agency. The one CPN who stated that he did not work with an open referral system, stated that he would accept clients from any source, but 'medical cover' would have to be gained first. This meant that no client could be accepted without either the consultant psychiatrist or the client's general practitioner knowing about the CPN's involvement. The psychiatrist or general practitioner 'knowing' about the client appeared to be taken by the CPN to mean that there was tacit agreement for treatment to be offered.

There is an apparent indiscriminate acceptance of all referrals by the CPNs. That is, all the referrals were accepted as clients in the sense that they were included in the CPNs' case load numbers (albeit that some were discharged after a relatively short period of time, or were categorised as 'inactive').

None of the CPNs gave the reason for accepting a new referral as having been the result of a formal assessment. Formal assessment forms were used in two of the four teams, but even when they were used they

Table 5: Reasons given by the CPNs for Accepting the Referrals (Q.72 of the Diary-interview Schedule)

Value label	Value	Frequency	Percent	Cum. percent
Arbitrary	1	123	48.8	48.8
Interesting	2	7	2.8	51.6
Speciality	3	5	2.0	53.6
Delegation/request	4	35	13.9	67.5
Appropriate	5	58	23.0	90.5
CMHT	6	3	1.2	91.7
Other	9	5	2.0	93.7
Re-referral	10	16	6.3	100.0
Total		252	100.0	

were not referred to as a justification for continuing to be involved with the client, for stopping involvement, or for re-referring the client to another health care professional.

On only five occasions (2%) did the CPNs state that they had accepted the referral because they believed that they had the specialist skills to deal with the issues for which the referrer had indicated the client needed help, or the CPNs themselves decided were the client's problem/illness.

Seven (2.8%) of the referrals were accepted by the CPNs because they believed the individual would be 'interesting to work with'. The CPNs appeared to conclude this after reading the details on the referral form, having had a conversation with the referrer, or following their initial contact with the client.

The CPNs reported that they had accepted only three clients (1.2%) as a result of being identified during CMHT discussions as the practitioners with the relevant skills or experience. However, when questioned in more depth, on one of these occasions, the CPN involved implied that the decision to accept the client was more to do with the number of clients he had on his case load, rather than whether he was competent to provide the appropriate treatment for the client:

Interviewer: 'Why did you take the referral, I mean why you rather than anybody else?'
CPN: 'I suppose, I mean apart from the informal thing of just generally knowing whether you feel, there's that kind of like unsaid thing of whether you know where you are with your case load.'

Sixteen (6.3%) of the referrals were accepted by the CPNs because they had been clients of that particular CPN service in the past. The client being known to the psychiatric services seemed to be taken as a valid reason for making contact and offering treatment. Thirty-five (13.9%)

clients were accepted on the basis that they were delegated (by another health care professional or a manager) to a named CPN. Nearly one-third of the clients that were referred in this way were from consultant psychiatrists.

The CPNs accepted 23% (n =58) of the referrals on the basis that they were 'appropriate', without further explanation. There were, however, a number of occasions when a referrer's good record of providing appropriate clients encouraged the CPN to accept subsequent referrals:

> Interviewer: 'Why did you accept him as a referral?'
> CPN: 'I accepted him because the GP, well, the GP who referred him, we'd had referrals in the past and the referrals he had gave us in the past had been appropriate referrals.'

Most significant of all, however, is that 48.8% (n = 123) of the referrals were contacted by the CPNs (and the vast majority then placed on their case loads) for reasons that I have described as 'arbitrary'. That is, for nearly half of the referrals, the CPNs provided a justification for accepting the referred individual that was incidental to such criteria as the apparent appropriateness of the referral, whether the CPN possessed the relevant skills, or whether the referral had been delegated to that particular CPN:

> Interviewer: 'Why did you accept her?'
> CPN: 'I don't know with this one, really. My turn, I suppose.'

The chance reasons for a CPN treating a client may suggest that CPNs are inherently generic and that the CPNs behave capriciously in determining who takes a particular referral because it doesn't matter which CPN provides treatment for which client.

Conversely, it could be interpreted as a less than well organised and effective approach to matching available resources to the perceived needs of the clients. However, even when the CPN decides that she or he has the specialist skills, knowledge and/or experience to provide treatment for a client, it does not always seem to be the result of some formal appraisal, but merely the CPN's own opinion of her or his abilities, or again the product of relatively arbitrary processes:

> Interviewer: 'Why did you accept the referral?'
> CPN: 'Um [5 sec. pause] I tend to take ladies with depression and anxiety problems.'

Accepting a referral, therefore, appears to be dependent on factors other than the objective testing of a client's suitability to enter into the psychiatric system.

Constructing Case Loads

In this section, I explore further the ways in which the CPNs in the study organise their case loads. What became of interest during the research was not just how the characteristics of the CPNs' case loads were affected by their subjective and undiscerning acceptance of clients, but the other ways in which they construct their workload. That is, it became apparent when talking with the CPNs that they had a considerable amount of freedom to influence the size and shape of their case loads.

As has been mentioned, a number of clients, with whom all active involvement by the CPN had ceased, were kept on her or his case load. In the following quotation from one of the CPNs, the client appears to exist in a therapeutic twilight zone: 'He [the client] is like not formally on my case load ... Although I saw him, I assessed him and I've written to his GP ... but I haven't put him formally on my case load, I haven't taken him on ... After having said that, I will be visiting him. Kind of like, formally, he's not on my case load, but informally he is.'

Retaining clients 'informally' may be a useful way of ensuring that if individuals require urgent treatment then they can be seen by the CPN without either party becoming involved in time-consuming bureaucratic referral procedures. In this sense, it is advantageous for the client as she or he may be visited more quickly than would otherwise be possible, even under the guarantees of the Patient's Charter. Furthermore, in these circumstances, the client would be treated by someone who has been involved with her or his case.

The CPN may also be acting in the client's interest by preventing the stigma associated with a formal psychiatric career. However, the collection of semi-official clients is an example of the insidious social control function of mental health nursing. That is, it perpetuates the surveillance and psychiatric career of certain clients (perhaps even without their knowledge) prior to and/or beyond the period when they have had formal contact with the mental health services. Unlike the recognised dangers associated with official measures of social control, such as 'supervision registers' and supervised aftercare (Bean, 1993; Eastman, 1994), this process is covert and unregulated. Therefore, it could be described as a greater abuse of human rights because it is not open to public scrutiny.

Most interesting of all was how the construction of the CPNs' case loads and the creation of psychiatric careers for those individuals referred to the CPNs was influenced by the CPN's decision to either visit or not visit the general practitioners' surgeries: 'I try to control the amount of referrals, you know, from the GPs, I get by not visiting their surgeries so often' (CPN).

The rate of referrals being sent to the CPNs by the general practitioners depends to a significant extent, therefore, on the number of times the surgeries are attended. Furthermore, certain general practitioners are targeted by the CPNs when new referrals are required to increase case loads – i.e. those who have a track record of supplying what the CPNs perceive as 'appropriate' clients.

It would appear that frivolous decisions made by nurses have the effect of increasing or decreasing the pool of those people who are categorised as 'mentally ill'. However, the CPNs' actions may be the consequence of a lack of assertiveness identifiable with nursing's traditional position in the occupational hierarchy. Whereas one CPN stated that he could 'always say no', most indicated that they found great difficulty in refusing openly to accept a referral on to their case loads. One of the CPN managers expressed concern over the pressure some nurses allow themselves to be put under from the general practitioners: 'CPNs often find it difficult to say no – and that comes from all sorts of reasons, for example, having such a really good, firm relationship with the GP and the GP's feeling really lost, the CPN's got 34 people on the case load and really can't manage any more, but the GP's saying: "Look, I'm really in the cart here" and it's pretty easy to say yes and it's quite difficult to say no.'

That is, although referrals could still be delivered, for example, by post, CPNs may moderate their physical attendance at a general practitioner's surgery as a method of avoiding direct pressure to take on more clients.

Another aspect concerning the construction of case loads is connected with what happens when the CPNs are on holiday or are absent from work due to sickness. Three of the CPNs were on sick leave for a number of weeks while I was obtaining the data for this study and obviously holidays were taken. Incredibly, virtually none of the clients with whom the CPNs were involved actively were contacted by their mental health colleagues when holidays or sickness occurred. This was despite explicit assurances from the CPNs that they did 'cover' for each other during these periods. Deputisation for CPNs who were sick or on holiday didn't appear to occur even when they were away from work for considerable periods.

For example, one CPN had been on holiday for three weeks and had been back at work for another week before the research interview took place. There was no evidence that two clients from this CPN's case load (who, previously, had been visited regularly) had been contacted by any other mental health worker for these four weeks. In another instance, a CPN, who had been on sick leave for about a month, pointed to a pile of case records relating to 'active' clients and complained: 'See, I had all of these schizophrenics when I left [on sick leave], they're still here.'

Interestingly, one of the clients who had not been contacted during this CPN's absence, was reported to have 'got better' without receiving any treatment from anyone and was consequently to be discharged!

This situation raises the question of just how necessary are mental health workers, if not providing their therapy results in spontaneous cures? Could withholding treatment be a bizarre example of 'paradoxical intervention' (i.e. doing the opposite of what might seem to be the most suitable course of action) or are clients being maintained on case loads for reasons other than those that relate directly to their mental health needs?

Furthermore, the amount of direct contact the CPNs had with their clients during normal working periods is surprisingly low (Table 6). The CPNs had no direct contact for 59% (n = 1006) of the accumulative number of weeks (n = 1712) that data were collected on the 252 referrals in the study. Moreover, the CPNs had no other involvement (e.g. telephone conversations with the client, or with the referrer) for 70.3% (n = 1203) of the weeks.

Table 6: Time spent by the CPNs on Direct Contact with Clients (Q.73 of the Diary-interview Schedule)

Value label	Value	Frequency	Percent	Cum percent
None	1	1006	58.8	58.8
Less than one hour	2	319	18.6	77.4
One hour or more, less than two	3	372	21.7	99.1
Two hours or more	4	15	0.9	100.0
Total		1712	100.0	

The lack of direct contact may indicate that clients do not require personal contact with the CPNs on a weekly basis. However, there is no evidence that the decision to meet or not meet with a client is made through an objective evaluation of needs. Alternatively, it could be that an ineffective delivery of care is connected to problems of resourcing. That is, it could be that the CPNs are over-stretched and can only manage to have a limited number of meetings with a client. Another explanation might be, as suggested above, that many clients are kept on the CPNs' case loads who don't need to be there, who could be discharged or might not have needed to be labelled as mentally ill in the first place. Furthermore, as has been mentioned already (and is discussed again below) a number of clients who the CPNs intended to discharge (and with whom all active involvement had ceased) were unintentionally left on their case loads. In addition to this, the CPNs admitted that they occasionally accepted clients for the primary reason of fostering good relationships with general practitioners and consultant psychiatrists.

The data indicate, therefore, that CPNs organise their case loads by various methods that are not always connected with the individual requirements of their actual or potential clients. In doing so, they demonstrate the existence of a form of clinical autonomy that I wish to describe as 'de facto'. Furthermore, the CPNs are not exercising legitimate freedom of action over their practice, but are covertly constructing the conditions under which they work.

Discussions with Colleagues

The issue of the CPNs consulting with other mental health professionals about the treatment of their clients is considered in this section. What is of interest with reference to clinical autonomy is how often the CPNs discussed their clients with general practitioners, members of the CMHT, supervisors and managers. That is, if the CPNs do not confer with colleagues or managers about their work, then this may imply a high degree of clinical autonomy.

What became obvious early on in the study was that the CPNs did not appear to talk regularly with colleagues or managers with regard to any aspect of their work with the clients on their case loads. For 67% (n = 1147) of the weeks reviewed in the study (n = 1712), the CPNs did not discuss the clients with anyone at all. That is, in less than one-third of the weeks covered in the research (n = 565) did the CPNs communicate directly with, for example a colleague, about the assessment, treatment, prognosis or discharge of the 252 new clients. The CPNs had the greatest number of discussions with the general practitioners (20.5%; n = 156) and then the consultant psychiatrists (12.9%; n = 98). This was to be expected given that these two groups provided the majority of the referrals.

With respect to indirect communication, the CPNs and their managers stated that it was necessary to supply a new client's general practitioner with a letter indicating what treatment was being offered and another letter when the client was discharged. This procedure also applied to the client's psychiatrist if one was, or had been, involved. However, on only 51 occasions did the CPNs report that this had happened.

Statistical tests of association on the data indicate there is a significant relationship between the referral source and whether or not discussions were held (n = 1712; df = 11; p < 0.05; Pearson's Chi-Square = < 0.00001; Phi < 0.00001; Cramer's V = < 0.00001). Of the number of weeks in which discussions took place (n = 565), the client being discussed had been referred by a general practitioner in 38.8% of the weeks (n = 219) and a consultant psychiatrist in 15.9% (n = 90) of the weeks. Therefore, this confirms that where the psychiatrists or general practitioners referred a client, discussions were more likely to occur. However, the ratio of weeks when discussions were held to weeks when no discussions were held for referrals made by consultant psychiatrists is 1:2.5 compared with 1:1.7 for those referrals made by general practitioners. That is, the clients who had been referred by the consultant psychiatrist were less likely to be discussed by the CPNs than those referred by the general practitioners.

The next most frequent set of discussions were with other CPNs. These were held on 87 (11.4.%) occasions. This, however, is a very low figure considering that all but one of the CPNs shared an office with at least one other CPN. That is, it could be assumed that informal discussions about clients would be an inevitable occurrence where CPNs met regularly in the working environment, but the data suggest that this is not the case.

Discussions with staff belonging to the psychiatric medical teams (apart from the consultant psychiatrists) were held on 55 occasions (7.2%). Conferment took place between the CPNs and occupational therapists on 43 (5.7%) occasions, with social workers on 22 (2.9.%) and psychologists on 10 (1.3%). Managers were consulted in 12 (1.6%) instances and supervisors in only two (0.3%).

A significant association is also indicated between the clients' diagnoses, as reported by the CPNs and whether discussions were held or not held (n = 1712; df = 14; p < 0.05; Pearson's Chi-Square = 0.00318; Phi 0.00318; Cramer's V 0.00318). Clients with the following sets of symptoms were discussed the most: anxiety and/or depression; delusions and/or hallucinations; 'problems with living'.

Of the number of weeks that discussions took place for all of the clients (n = 565), 43.9% (n = 248) involved clients suffering from anxiety and/or depression. The number of weeks the clients with these symptoms were involved in the study was 620. Therefore, discussions took place on 40% of the weeks available (ratio of 1:2.5).

For those clients who were described as suffering from delusions and/or hallucinations, discussions were held on 101 weeks. This represents 17.9% of the total number of weeks discussions were held for all categories of clients. However, it is 35.7% of the number of weeks the clients in this category were monitored in the research (n = 283; ratio of 1:2.8).

Discussions were held regarding clients described as having 'problems with living' on 66 occasions. This represents 11.7% of the total number of weeks that discussions occurred. The number of weeks that clients with this label were monitored, however, was only 92. Therefore, these clients were discussed for 71% of the available weeks (ratio of 1:1.4). That is, clients reported to be suffering from the non-medicalised classification of 'problems with living' were much more likely to be discussed than those in any other category.

Although significant relationships have been found between the client's diagnosis and the referral agent and whether or not discussions were held, this was not repeated with respect to the CPNs' accounts of why they accepted the referrals. That is, there appears to be no association between the reasons given by the CPNs for deciding to provide treatment for the clients who became part of their case load and the number of discussions that were to occur subsequently.

Two hundred and fifty (32.9%) of the total number of discussions were held with a group of people other than colleagues or managers – relatives of the client, neighbours and, most frequently (n = 125), student nurses on placement in the community. That is, the people to whom the CPNs talk to most about their practice are trainees, not their colleagues in the CMHTs and certainly not their managers or their supervisors.

The overall lack of discussion did not seem to concern the CPNs. Indeed, they appeared to deceive themselves about how much contact they actually had with colleagues as they often stated that it was their normal practice to consult constantly with, for example, the consultant psychiatrists, general practitioners or the membership of the CMHT as a whole, before accepting or discharging a client. As the data indicate (from the CPNs' own accounts of what they did with each specific client) this did not happen.

Other members of the CMHT are not under any such misapprehension. The psychiatrists, in particular, complained that the CPNs did not make themselves for discussion. However, in turn, the CPNs criticised the consultant psychiatrists for not always being accessible. These problems in communication led to autonomous decisions being made. In this next quotation, a CPN explains that when the consultant psychiatrist cannot be contacted, unilateral decisions are made and, at a later date, the consultant is informed of what action has been taken:

> CPN: 'I tried to contact the consultant, but it's very difficult, so I did leave a message with his secretary.'
> Interviewer: 'Is that a common problem, not being able to get direct contact with the consultant?'
> CPN: 'It is recently. We sometimes see him in team meetings, but it's a big problem.'
> Interviewer: 'So if you want something sorted out fairly quickly?'
> CPN: 'Sometimes we have difficulty ... what I've found what I am doing is making a decision, then informing them of it, rather than I'd like to discuss it with them. If the contact is difficult, then the only way is to make a decision and let them know and then see what the comeback is really.'

Autonomy here is yet again by default. The CPN is not being pro-active in exercising clinical freedom. The CPN is reacting to a situation in which it is difficult to do anything but act without consultation with the psychiatrist. Furthermore, the desire of the CPN to engage in a dialogue with the psychiatrist in the first place implies that 'permission' is sought to carry out if not all then certainly some forms of action. Moreover, the notion of 'comeback', suggests the CPN is not awaiting feedback from an equal, but feels vulnerable to admonishment from a superior.

Discharge and Admission

The procedures used by the CPNs when discharging clients from their case loads is examined in this section. Reference is also made to how the CPNs organise the admission of clients to psychiatric hospitals (or psychiatric units within general hospitals). If a CPN is able to stop treating clients and can expedite the entry of clients into in-patient facilities, without recourse to colleagues, supervisors or managers, then she or he could be considered to have a high degree of clinical independence.

Very few of the clients in the study became in-patients during the period of data collection (n = 2). However, 81 (32.1%) were discharged. A further 29 (11.5%) were re-referred to another professional in the field of mental health and were subjected to a similar process to that involved in the discharge of clients.

Of the 40 clients referred by consultant psychiatrists, 30% (n = 12) were discharged or re-referred. Where the general practitioners were the referrers, discharged or re-referred clients accounted for 39.8% (n = 39) of their 98 referrals. However, much higher percentages of the clients referred by hospital nurses and staff of residential homes (48%; n = 20) and of those referred by CPNs (50%; n = 8) were discharged or re-referred. Self-referrals who were discharged or re-referred during the course of the study reached a high 73.8% (n = 14).

There would seem to be a trend, therefore, for referrals made by the consultants and general practitioners to be maintained on the CPNs' case loads for much longer periods than clients referred by other agencies (including self-referrals). This discrepancy cannot be accounted for by the type of problems these client groups were identified by the referrers and CPNs as having, or by the expectations of the referrers, or by the reasons for accepting the referrals given by the CPNs.

A plausible explanation is that deference is given to the perceived legitimacy of referrals made by the consultant psychiatrists and general practitioners compared with other referrers. That is, the CPNs may keep referrals on their case loads for longer because of the status of these particular referrers.

However, a more pertinent question (in relation to clinical autonomy) is, do the CPNs confer with, or ask permission from, other members of the CMHT, the general practitioners or managers, before making major decisions about the careers of their clients? In particular, do the CPNs consult with anyone before discharging a client, or before organising the admission of a client as an in-patient of a psychiatric hospital?

As we have seen above, the CPNs did not discuss their clients regularly with colleagues. This lack of discussion relates also to the topic of discharge (although a different picture emerges with regard to admission). Almost without exception, the CPNs in this study made the decision to discharge and frequently carried out the discharge, without discussion with any other colleague. Moreover, any discussion that took place happened after the decision to discharge the client had been made. The consultant psychiatrist and general practitioner are told of the CPN's intention to discharge the client, or are informed of the discharge after it has occurred.

Many of the CPNs' colleagues were very critical of the way in which clients were discharged, as the following quotation from one of the consultant psychiatrists illustrates: 'I'd prefer to be informed before it's done. Ideally, I like to get the message, "I think this person is ready for discharge and I'd like to discuss it with you", rather than somebody phoning me and saying: "I've discharged Fred Bloggs".'

Decisions to discharge were taken not only without any discussion with colleagues, but also no formal or objective criteria were reported to have been used to evaluate the effects of the treatment or readiness of the client for discharge. That is, as with a significant proportion of the reasons given for accepting clients, decisions to discharge appeared to be subjective and arbitrary:

> Interviewer: 'What did you do for that three-quarters of an hour [with the client]?'
> CPN: 'We reviewed what we'd done and what had happened since I'd met him and if there was any more to be done and I discharged him.'

Moreover, bureaucratic conveniences influenced the exact timing of an impending discharge, rather than it being based on clinical judgement. Here, the length of a client's psychiatric career depended on when the CPN decided to complete the relevant paperwork and, in particular, when the organisation required the nursing staff to complete statistical (computerised and/or written) accounts of their practice: 'As a general rule, I would probably have discharged her at the end of this week, or the end of next week, but all the people I want to discharge will have to wait 'til ... I get round to doing all the notes' (CPN).

The subjective and unilateral judgement of the CPN was influential also with regard to getting a client admitted as a psychiatric in-patient. In the following quotation, the CPN does consult with the psychiatrist. However, the opinion of the CPN seems to have been taken at face value:

Interviewer: 'Did you initiate him going in to hospital?'
CPN: 'Yeh, yeh.'
Interviewer: 'How did you do that?'
CPN: 'Well, I just contacted the medical staff at [the psychiatric hospital] and just discussed the situation as he's on the out-patient list. I'd spoke with [the consultant] and a bed was available and er that was simply that.'

In situations where the CPN believed admission to be necessary, she or he suggested techniques that enabled this to happen in a way which meant that any potential obstacle could be circumvented. For example, one obstacle may be the unavailability of the consultant psychiatrist, whose agreement for the admission of a client is usually required. However, the CPN is not unduly hindered: 'If we go and see someone, we ring the ward and say: "Have you got a bed? We are bringing someone in, can you tell the consultant", otherwise you spend hours trying to get the consultant' (CPN).

Once again, therefore, the CPN appears to be operating with a freedom in her or his work that allows significant actions to be taken without any interference from members of the CMHT or the managers. However, as with other areas of the CPN's practice, this could be viewed not so much as a display of genuine clinical autonomy, but as an example of role-deviation because she or he is expected to consult with others.

Content of Contact

In this section, the CPNs' accounts of what happened when they made direct contact with their new clients is examined. Particular attention is paid to the subject of the CPNs' assessment of the mental state of their clients. Also, through the evaluation of the terminology used to describe the events that occurred during these face-to-face sessions with clients, the CPNs' ideological affiliations are assessed.

The CPNs made direct contact with the clients in this study on 706 occasions. On 280 (40%) of these occasions, the approach taken was described by the CPNs as one of offering 'reassurance', 'support', or 'counselling'. There was a concentration on 'medication' (e.g. giving injections of anti-psychotic drugs; ensuring prescribed treatment was being taken; observing for side-effects) in 18% (n = 126) of the sessions.

The implementation of a specialist therapy (e.g. 'desensitisation') occurred on 66 (9.4%) occasions and the CPN offering specific advice about the client's condition or treatment occurred on 63 (9%) occasions. Educating the client (e.g. about her or his diet or 'illness') accounted for 11 (1.6%) of the sessions and the evaluation of the treatment the client had received from the CPN on seven (1%).

The CPNs asserted many times in the Diary-interviews that for the first session with a client they would assess her or his mental state and what course of action to take (if any) in the future. Twenty-nine (66%) of the 44 clients who the referrers had asked specifically to be assessed by the CPN were seen in the first week after the referral was made. Of these, 23 (79%) were described by the CPNs as having been assessed. However, out of the 71.2% (n = 178) of the clients monitored in the study who were seen in the first week, only 60% (n = 107) of these were assessed, according to the CPNs' own elaborate versions of what they did during these initial sessions. What is more significant is that on only 20.2% (n = 141) of the total number of occasions when direct contact occurred, did the CPNs indicate they had assessed the client. If the CPNs were assessing each client then this figure should have been, at the very least, the same as the number of clients in the study (i.e. 252) and probably much higher given the CPNs' claims that they may take more than one week to complete the task of assessment.

Moreover, the content of the interaction in the encounter described as 'assessment' is worth further examination. In the following extract, the CPN deliberately avoids using any pre-organised schedule in the assessment and planning of treatment for the client. Instead, the CPN initiates an approach that approximates to entering into the relationship with the client *tabula rasa*. However, there is inconsistency in the CPN's method. Although the assessment form is blank, the CPN admits harbouring a number of unidentified 'categories' into which the client's responses may be placed: 'It's a blank piece of paper right in front of me, um but I suppose um, with categories in the back of my mind.'

In this next extract, far from adopting any systematic method of history-taking, the CPN states quite openly that 'instinct' is the predominant quality used in the assessment of a new client: 'Usually, I have some sort of instinct of what I will do and get some feedback from the client about "this is what happened" and "this is where I'd like to go" and "what I'd like to do" and sometimes even "this is how I'd like you to help". So, usually, there is some direction from them or I can initiate some sort of movement, perhaps clarify some things and start moving them in certain directions.'

Where a written assessment form is adopted by the CPNs, there appears to be little standardisation in its use. For example, in one team where forms are available they are not used by all members of the team. The CPNs in this team gave the impression that they could be very flexible in the way they proceeded with the assessment documentation if they did decide to use it and portrayed intuitiveness and experience as robust 'professional' techniques in the appraisal of a client's mental condition.

The problem with the otherwise admirable qualities of 'instinct' and 'intuition', however, is that they are not integral to contemporary nursing ideology. Today's nursing theorists advocate the methodical and scientific formulation of health care practice. For example, with reference to mental health nursing, Paquette et al. (1991) describe procedures for nursing diagnosis and the systematic planning of treatment. Kalman and Waughfield (1993) list a number of 'standards' that they recommend for psychiatric nursing. These include: 'The nurse applies appropriate theory that is scientifically sound as a basis for decisions regarding nursing practice … The nurse continuously collects data that are comprehensive, accurate and systematic… The nurse utilises nursing diagnosis … to express conclusions supported by recorded assessment data and current scientific premises' (p13).

Furthermore, decisions based on instinct and intuition cannot easily be inspected and challenged by the CPNs' peers or mentors in the same way as preformulated and 'scientific' assessment inventories can be. Nor are they conducive to the present fixation of nurse theoreticians with the manufacture of 'reflective practitioners' (Reed and Proctor, 1993; Palmer et al., 1994). That is, 'reflective' actions cannot be based merely on unfettered innate or experiential learning.

Kelly and Field (1994) point out that it is a caricature of the medical profession to suggest that its members believe in a unidirectional and biochemical oriented explanation for ill health. They argue, for example, that medicine has incorporated many social aspects in the diagnosis and treatment of illness. However, the CPNs in this study displayed an unfaltering allegiance to values that have their roots in the more narrow definition of the 'medical model'. That is, in conversation about their work, the CPNs used words and phrases consonant with organic aetiology and traditional psychiatric labels. For example, they assiduously used such expressions as 'endogenous depression', 'neurotic depression', 'psychosis', 'fixed delusional belief' and 'schizophrenia'.

The continued use of medical concepts indicates the precarious position of mental nursing with reference to medical dominance. Moreover, the reliance on subjective criteria in clinical judgements weakens further the case for professionalisation, particularly when confronted with the present developments in positivistic psychiatry.

Team Membership

It has been a premise of the research study described here that membership of a CMHT may change the CPN's clinical practice. Specifically, the entry into the team could have an effect on how autonomous the CPN can be in making clinical decisions. When asked the question 'What makes a good CPN?', the tension between clinical autonomy and team membership was unveiled by one of the occupational therapists interviewed in the study: 'I think someone who can work in a team, which I think is the problem – I don't think a lot of CPNs do … they work too autonomously.'

For this team member, CPNs have a problem in relinquishing some degree (if not all) of their assumed independence.

In all four teams participating in this research there was considerable confusion about both the functions and status of the CMHT and the roles of its participants. For example, 'leaders' were never identified expressly in any of the teams. In two of the teams, the term 'coordinator' was used to describe the person who accepted the responsibility of arranging and acting as chairperson for meetings, but who held no authority to direct the practice of the other members.

With respect to leadership, the opinions of the consultant psychiatrists were unequivocal. These quotations from two different psychiatrists demonstrate the point well: 'Every team has a captain and the consultant psychiatrist should be the captain'; 'I think the consultant is the person to actually lead a team, which includes the CPNs'.

Moreover, the CPNs were expected by their colleagues to explain what treatment they were providing to their clients at weekly meetings of the CMHT. However, a 'review' of the CPNs' clients at these meeting did not take place very often, a state of affairs that caused one psychologist considerable consternation:

'They [the CPNs] can say they are discharging a client in the team meeting, but there's not an effective check made as to whether or not this is right. CPNs do have control over this. There is an absurd kind of lip service paid to discussing it. You don't get time to discuss when there are 10 professionals sitting around, so it's just a case of this is the way it is. Unless the psychiatrist is very involved or one of the other professionals knows the client really well there is no real checking.'

Here there is an assumption by the psychologist that it is the psychiatrist's role to direct the work of the CPN. However, as indicated in the quotation above, there is no formalised examination of the CPNs' clinical work at the team meetings. Generally, therefore, membership of the team does not inhibit the CPNs from organising their working day as they wish. It does not, for example, impinge on their decisions about how many clients they will visit, nor on whom they wish to consult with (if anyone) about the treatment they believe to be suitable for their clients. That is, most of the time the nurses decide for themselves the content and structure of their practice without any liaison with a supervisor, manager or colleague.

This freedom of action does, of course, have certain parameters. For example, where CPNs share an office and/or operate from a building with colleagues and a manager, then this will affect their behaviour. It is axiomatic, however, that nurses working in the community do not come under the observation of their colleagues, or the scrutiny of their managers, to anything like the extent that they do when they work inside a hospital. Moreover, computer records do not necessarily provide a valid audit of the performance of community staff. Hunt and Mangan (1990), referring to CPN services, acknowledge that, at present, community nurses regard the information obtained through computerised records 'as giving limited, if not distorted, pictures of their work' (p95).

A certain amount of managerial overseeing was carried out in one of the centres in this study. The CPNs were expected to record in a communal diary if they left the building and the time of any appointments they had with their clients. In another centre, the CPNs wrote on a centrally placed whiteboard what their activities were going to be for each day of the week. However, as with computer records, the information supplied would obviously depend on the CPNs' willingness to account accurately for their actions.

Notwithstanding these self-reporting records of the CPNs' movements (and the example explored below of the manager accompanying the CPN on one day every few months), the observation of the CPN by her or his peers, colleagues or managers only occurs for a small proportion of the working day. The CPN has the opportunity to spend most of her or his time either with clients or travelling to and from appointments and therefore can avoid easily the 'gaze' of colleagues, peers and managers.

These factors could, therefore, be viewed as demonstrating the CPN's ability to exercise clinical autonomy. However, gauged by such factors as the reactions of the other members of the team, it is problematic to look on this as a licit *modus operandi* for CPNs.

Supervision

'Clinical supervision for CPNs has always been a big issue and one that I think has never been properly addressed' (nurse manager).

One of the most important influences on the clinical autonomy of any practitioner is supervision. That is, if work is not overseen at all, or supervised from within the practitioner's discipline, then it could be argued that clinical autonomy is possible. If, on the other hand, the work of the practitioner is supervised by members of another discipline or managers (particularly if compulsory), then the potential for professionalisation is limited, if not completely unobtainable. In this section, the way in which the work of the 10 CPNs in the study was supervised and the views of the members of the CMHTs and the managers on the issue of supervision, are evaluated.

The supervision of health care practitioners has become a major concern internationally (Severinsson, 1995). In the United Kingdom, there is much discussion about how to incorporate supervision into nursing practice (Jones, 1996; Morcom and Hughes, 1996). There are, however, numerous definitions of supervision (Hawkins and Shohet, 1989; Wilkin in Butterworth and Faugier, 1992; DoH, 1994b). Two of the most obvious are, first, the form of interaction connected with managerial control and second, the type associated with the reviewing of clinical work in order to help the personal development and/or skills of the practitioner being supervised.

Although in this study there was little clarity about what sort of supervision should be adopted (and whether or not it should be intradisciplinary or interdisciplinary), most of the CPNs, their colleagues and the managers, regarded the supervision of clinical work to be important. When interviewing the CPNs, I was interested not only in discovering what type of supervision they undertook, but whether it was available on an informal or formal basis. I use the terms 'formal' and 'informal' to differentiate between regular, pre-organised (and usually obligatory) sessions with an identified supervisor and *ad hoc* discussions with any available colleague.

In the early part of the study, six of the 10 CPNs stated that they received formal supervision from one of their colleagues in the CMHT or from a manager. All 10 of the CPNs in the study stated that they undertook frequent informal supervision on demand, usually from another CPN (especially if sharing an office with that CPN), but occasionally from a colleague who belonged to one of the other occupational groups. However, contradicting the initial impression given by the CPNs, the data from the whole of the study indicate that formal supervision (managerial or developmental) was provided on only two occasions. This astonishingly low figure represents 0.3% of the total number of discussions that were held by the CPNs with other colleagues or managers. The CPNs did report that they had discussed their clients a further 12 times with their managers, but the content of these discussions was not stated to be related specifically to supervision.

Furthermore, later in the study, the CPNs admitted that although supervision officially was expected to take place, it generally did not. From my own observations, the CPNs do talk with other nursing colleagues in the team about their clients in a general way on many occasions. But, mostly, the clients are mentioned in conversations which cover other non-related topics. For example, a client's treatment or prognosis may be alluded to in the middle of a discussion about the CPNs' working conditions or personal circumstances. Therefore, it would be difficult to classify these communications as even 'informal' supervision. Indeed, the function of these conversations appeared to be concerned more with the requirement to communicate on a superficial level in communal situations in order to pre-empt or diffuse interpersonal tensions.

Although the majority of the members of the teams considered it necessary for CPNs to have their work supervised, they differed with regard to the question of who should provide the supervision. There was criticism, from the psychiatrists and psychologists (who represented themselves as the 'senior' members of the CMHTs) about the ability of nurse managers to offer effective supervision to the CPNs. The managers were not viewed as credible in their clinical experience. Furthermore, the psychiatrists, as self-appointed leaders of the CMHTs, saw a logic in being also mentors to the CPNs. However, neither of these disciplines appear to be committed to a complementary arrangement whereby nurses could be supervised and offer supervision in return, as this quotation demonstrates:

> 'What I've said here is that I could be a resource, that I would provide supervision if they [the CPNs] wanted it ... I had one CPN come to me and she suggested that I joined in to discuss some of my cases, but I said that I didn't really want to do that. That really wasn't my agenda. I get other people to do that for me' (psychologist).

The non-reciprocal supervision of members of one occupational group by members of another underlines the perception of the psychologists and psychiatrists that they belong to superior disciplines compared with their nursing (as well as other) colleagues. Moreover, the criticism of the capacity of the nurse manager to supervise the CPNs could be regarded as congruous with the psychologists' and consultant psychiatrists' view that they should adopt this role. That is, where managers have a nursing background (all had in this study), they may be considered by the dominant disciplines to be in a similar (subordinate) occupational position as the CPNs.

The role of the nurse manager in the supervising of CPNs who belong to a CMHT leads inevitably to the issues of accountability. The definition of accountability used here refers to the formal, contractual responsibilities an individual has with an organisation (Ovretveit, 1993). Individuals are accountable to one or more representatives of an organisation for the fulfilment of these responsibilities. Practitioners may also be accountable to a professional organisation (for CPNs, this would be the United Kingdom Central Council for Nursing, Health Visiting and Midwifery) which provides codes of conduct and/or ethical regulations.

Technically, CPNs are accountable to their line manager. However, membership of a CMHT encourages a blurring of lines of accountability because responsibilities are not (and were not in the four teams in this study) delineated precisely or officially. Moreover, although CPNs may be accountable to their line manager, when they work in a CMHT the supervision of their practice could be carried out by either a manager (who is not part of the team), the team leader (who could be the consultant psychiatrist), by another CPN, or by one of the other members of the team (e.g. an occupational therapist or social worker). What type of supervision is provided (i.e. either managerial or developmental), will depend on what is sought by the CPN in the first place (where it is voluntary) and on who carries it out.

The data from this research indicate that accountability to the team may mean that CPNs become answerable to, and succumb to supervision by, members of other disciplines – especially psychiatry. In the following quotation, the nurse manager concedes that the supervision of the work of CPNs is 'inadequate'. Furthermore, the manager hints at the scenario of psychiatrists supervising nurses as being a possibility because of 'traditional' ties between the two groups: 'I think generally the supervision of the CPNs is inadequate ... I'm conscious that CPNs, certainly in comparison to, say, social workers, have nothing like the degree of supervision. I suppose what they do have, by tradition, are fairly close working relationships with medical staff which, to some extent, compensate.'

This manager is also drawing attention to the discrepancy between the organisation of intradisciplinary supervision for social workers and the scarcity of any such internal system of supervision for the CPNs in this study. Consequently, compared with social workers, it is more probable that the CPNs will lose the freedom they have (and fall prey to the hegemonic tendencies of the medical profession), if, and when, the issue of accountability is addressed in the CMHTs. These arrangements would then provide an irresistible model for psychiatric nurses working in hospitals.

Hierarchy

The clinical autonomy of mental health nurses working in the CMHTs is challenged seriously by the existence of interprofessional hierarchical structures. A hierarchical structure permeates the four teams in this study. This structure is embodied in the belief of the psychiatrists that they are (or should be) the leaders of the CMHTs and the view of psychologists and psychiatrists that they are an elite occupational caste. It is manifest also in the statements by the psychiatrists and psychologists that nurses should help to sustain the work of the 'senior' disciplines. Furthermore, the disempowering actions of the CPNs themselves reflect and promote the tacit mandate of these disciplines to dominate the CMHT.

In this next quotation, one of the psychologists states that her role in supervising nurses is of particular importance in the treatment of people who are suffering from acute mental illness. She voices her concern about the capabilities of CPNs to deliver such specialist treatment as, for example, cognitive therapy. The CPNs need to be supervised, she suggests, to stop them doing 'crackers things' and to prevent her own discipline from being held in disrepute. Furthermore, she recommends that the role of the CPNs should be confined to one of providing 'support':

> 'I think a lot of the work they [CPNs] do should be done by psychologists and I see my role as supervising and making sure they're not doing crackers things and giving psychological services a bad name. They always say they're doing cognitive therapy, and I don't think they know what cognitive therapy is ... I do think if they could stick to more supportive stuff and be ready to report back when more specialist help is needed and avoid getting out of their depth ... I think they give the psychologists a bad name because they call it therapy.'

Hughes (1971) has referred to nursing as an occupation that undertakes the 'dirty work' of health care. Similarly, psychiatric nurses may be expected to shoulder the mundane chores of the psychiatric services. However, taking on menial duties could have positive consequences for CPNs, as some degree of autonomy may be procured. That is, the payoff for accepting the role of providing support to psychiatry and psychology could be that the CPNs avoid direct interference (or 'supervision') from their colleagues. It is only when the CPNs are perceived to be penetrating areas of work considered to be the remit of psychiatry and psychology that they are liable to inspection by the 'senior' professionals.

It could be argued, therefore, that the senior groups offer the CPNs a stable system of occupational relationships based on paternalism and patronage. The CPNs encourage a solicitous relationship with the consultant psychiatrists through their internalisation of the medical discourse. Deference towards medicine is encouraged further by the CPNs insisting that each client on their case load has a 'responsible medical practitioner' (who may be either a consultant psychiatrist or a general practitioner).

However, the key criterion used to distinguish senior from junior disciplines in the CMHT is the perceived ability of an occupational group to perform effectively the 'diagnosis' of a client's mental condition. In this quotation, a consultant psychiatrist suggests that his assessment procedures, compared with those of the mental health nurses, are more complex and comprehensive: 'The depth and sophistication is going to be different [between] the CPN and a consultant psychiatrist, and it's better for the consultant to do it more thoroughly.'

Freidson has pointed to the medical profession's 'prerogative to diagnose' (1970b, p141). In this study, four of the five consultant psychiatrists, and all the psychologists, indicated that they considered this to be the fundamental element in the demarcation between the senior and the junior groups of occupations in the CMHT.

Conflict

Conflict between the various members of the CMHTs occurred in a number of different ways. As has been found in other studies (e.g. Onyett et al., 1994), much of this conflict is centred on the actual or potential dominance of the team by the consultant psychiatrist.

A large part of the discord between the CPNs and consultant psychiatrists relates to the issue of an 'open' referral system. This system, supported by the nursing management, encourages a high rate of referrals to be sent directly to the CPNs from general practitioners and thereby reduces the psychiatrists' sphere of influence over the work of the CPNs. It was contended by the consultant psychiatrists that such a system created difficulties identifying who had medical responsibility for the client.

However, the CPNs are in a double bind situation with respect to medical responsibility and clinical autonomy. On the one hand, nine of the ten CPNs stated that they wanted to accept whichever clients they find appropriate and from whatever source. But on the other hand, all of the CPNs want the consultant psychiatrist or the general practitioner to accept 'medical' responsibility. The responsibility referred to here by the CPNs appeared to be a euphemism for 'ultimate' liability. That is, in the final analysis, the medical staff would be expected to 'carry the can' for the clients on the CPN's case load.

This, of course, also puts the consultant psychiatrists into a double bind with respect to their occupational position in the CMHT. The consultant psychiatrists may inadvertently further CPN autonomy and reduce their own professional status if they do not accept medical responsibility for all of the clients (including those referred by general practitioners).

Some of the members of the CMHT suggested that, although an open system was acceptable, referrals sent directly to the CPNs should be reviewed by the team: '[The CPNs] should accept them [referrals] from anybody, but it should be decided among the team, really, as to who's taking what' (social worker).

Concern was expressed also by the psychiatrists about the number of 'worried well' clients received by the CPN from general practitioners. This, it was suggested, displaced attention being given to clients suffering from serious mental disorder. Limited resources, the argument continued, must be concentrated on this latter group and the CMHT should act as a regulatory conduit to control the type of client treated by the psychiatric services.

One other major source of enmity between the nursing and medical staff in the CMHT relates to payments from the health authority for consultant psychiatrists undertaking 'domiciliary visits'. In one of the teams, there was much cynicism from the CPNs and their manager about the consultant psychiatrist being asked unnecessarily (as they viewed it) by general practitioners to see clients. Domiciliary visiting exemplifies the structural difference between CPNs and consultant psychiatrists. That is, the consultants' ascendant position, and that of the medical profession, is endorsed through the existence of 'domiciliary visits'. The system is activated by the medical profession (i.e. general practitioners) and serviced by the medical profession (i.e. consultant psychiatrists), to the exclusion of any other discipline in the CMHT.

Skulduggery

The CPNs are not wholly passive in their reaction to the dominating manoeuvres of the psychiatrists. During the interviews for this research, their response to the consultant psychiatrists stipulating what treatment they expected to be implemented was often one of expressed hostility. In the quotation below, the CPN recalls being asked by the consultant psychiatrist to visit a client who had 'absconded' from hospital after having been admitted following a suicide attempt. The consultant wanted the CPN to ensure that the client had not injured herself:

> 'I did two visits, neither of which was answered. So, I got back to the consultant and explained the situation and said: "I've been back twice, how many times would you like me to continue trying to trace this girl?" It seemed to me that I was going to have to clear up someone else's inefficiency, if you like. She'd been an in-patient in hospital, she'd taken an overdose, why wasn't she observed? Why wasn't she kept an eye on if she was at risk? I was annoyed, because I felt I was being used, if you like, and I also felt that it was an inappropriate referral for a CPN anyway. Why didn't they ring the social worker?'

As with the issue of medical responsibility, a double bind of the CPN's own making is assembled with respect to occupational status. That is, while complaining about being used by the consultant psychiatrist to 'clear up someone else's inefficiency', the CPN does not refuse the request. Whatever the moral argument for visiting the client in these circumstances, doing so has the effect of reinforcing the CPN's subservient role to the consultant psychiatrist. Moreover, the introduction of 'supervision registers' (NHS Management Executive, 1994) and the enforced repatriation into hospital care of some mentally ill people under the 1995 Mental Health (Patients in the Community) Act, underlines the capacity of the psychiatrist to dictate significant elements of the CPN's role.

The CPN quoted above, although angry at the supplications of the psychiatrist, did not indulge in open disagreement. However, as a number of researchers have observed (Stein, 1967; Wright, 1985; Hughes,

1988), although they avoid public rows, nurses use tactics that result in their gaining considerable influence over decision-making processes. Indeed, the CPNs in this study executed a number of skulduggerous contrivances in order to combat unwelcome control being exerted by the consultant psychiatrists, For example, although the CPN would indicate that she or he was conforming to the 'request' of the consultant, or willing to negotiate, another course of action was actually followed. One CPN stated that when given an 'inappropriate' referral by the psychiatrist, one or two visits are made to the client before she or he is discharged, rather than simply refusing to accept the client in the first place.

A more extreme form of skulduggery committed by the CPNs, in the pursuance of their own agenda, is to make the psychiatrists more tractable by the use of 'sweeteners'. Here, the CPN accepts a limited number of clients from the psychiatrist, although the former deems them not to be in need of treatment. This is done consciously in order to resolve possible future disputes in the CPN's favour. This technique was also used as a way of manipulating general practitioners. In what appeared to be quite a widespread activity, another CPN explained that the primary reason for accepting one particular client was to encourage a 'good relationship' with the referrer, a general practitioner.

However, it is questionable whether any of the skulduggery the CPNs undertook was at all effective in changing the power relationship between them and the consultant psychiatrists. Their tactics were undercover and therefore so were their successes – that is, both went unnoticed. Moreover, the CPNs in this study were not engaged in an organised confrontation with the medical staff with the aim of asserting their occupational credentials. They played a 'game' in which their role was to act like affronted and rebellious adolescents when directed by an authoritarian parent. As with other doctor-nurse games, the degree to which the dominance of the profession of medicine over the occupation of nursing is tempered is only marginal.

Role

'A lot of people are asking at the moment, "what is the role of the CPN?" I think a lot of people are starting to say "these are expensive people, what are they doing?"' (manager).

The role of the CPN, as described by the CPNs, their colleagues in the CMHT and their managers, is replete with imprecision and ambiguity. That is, the informants in the study were unable to provide a lucid definition of the part played by the CPN in mental health care. However, one common theme reported by the CPNs' colleagues, was that they considered a constituent of the role of the CPN was administering and monitoring medication and, in particular, the giving of major tranquillisers by injection to people suffering from long-term mental illness.

The CPNs were somewhat ambivalent about this aspect of their work. At times, especially when it was perceived as justified by the CPNs (for example, because it was believed that the mental condition of a 'known' client would deteriorate without medication), this task would be performed unquestioningly. However, at other times, they complained that they did not wish to be 'used' by the medical practitioners for this purpose. They argued that the administering of injections could be carried out by, for example, district nurses or nurses employed by general practitioners. The CPNs seemed to regard the giving of injections to the mentally ill as a waste of their expertise – an 'expertise' they failed consistently to define.

It has been argued for some time that CPNs are abandoning altogether their attachment to working with the chronically mentally ill (see, for example, Weleminsky, 1989). Much criticism was levelled at the CPNs in this study by psychiatrists about neglecting this group of clients, particularly those suffering from schizophrenia. It was suggested that the CPNs had become too embroiled with the client group described as the 'worried well'. The clients in this group are principally those who have been diagnosed as suffering from neurotic illnesses and who are often referred directly to the CPNs by general practitioners. A specific criticism from one psychiatrist was that the CPNs (and 'other' practitioners in the team) want to work only with 'interesting' and 'rewarding' clients, and not those who suffer from psychotic illness:

> 'It's great for CPNs to do, or other professionals to do, support groups for married mothers and things, which is fine, but here we've got a high percentage of chronic, severely mentally ill people and in my book they come first. The well people who are worried are in need of help but the chronically mentally ill have to come first because they're the most vulnerable basically ... what can happen is that all the exciting and interesting and rewarding things get done and the chronics get left to fester.'

This concern about the CPNs concentrating too much on primary prevention and referrals from general practitioners was echoed by one of the nurse managers. This manager described working with the chronically mentally ill as the 'bread and butter' of psychiatric nursing, an area of work that shouldn't be left behind because CPNs have got the 'skills that nobody else has got'.

The role of the CPN, therefore, although lacking in clarity, is perceived to encompass a number of exclusive facets. The CPN is identified by her or his colleagues with the giving and supervising of medication. Although the CPN is viewed as having steered away from treating the chronically mentally disturbed, this is considered still to be an area of work that the CPN should commandeer.

These expectations of the CPN imply a function for the CPN in the 'surveillance' of the mentally ill in the community. The role of the CPN as an ancillary agent of social control is endorsed by the consultant psychiatrists. The CPNs are viewed as 'front-line workers' who could monitor the mental state of those people who had already come into contact with the psychiatric services and report back to the primary agent of social control – the consultant psychiatrist: 'They're sort of an early warning system in that they're out there and they can pick up things which are going on at an early [stage]' (consultant psychiatrist); 'I suppose I also like to use them as policemen ... in the sense of dropping in on someone who I'm concerned about, just to have a chat with them and see how they are and flag-up problems' (consultant psychiatrist).

The description of the CPNs as 'policemen' (and presumably there are also 'policewomen') leaves little doubt as to their social control function as conceived by this consultant psychiatrist.

Summary

The analysis of the data identifies a number of core themes that relate to the aims of this study. With respect to the level of autonomy the CPN exercises over the referral process, the nurses in the study appear to organise their case loads in a way that can be characterised as arbitrary. That is, the CPNs do not ordinarily assess formally the needs of the clients and, in the main, do not receive (or do not accept) guidance from the referrers about what form of treatment may be appropriate. Furthermore, the CPNs would appear to discharge clients without any objective evaluation of how ready they are for this action to be taken.

The CPNs also adopt specific techniques (not necessarily conducive to the obvious requirements of the psychiatric services) to manipulate the size of their case loads. Moreover, the CPNs do not discuss their clients on a regular basis with the person who made the referral in the first instance, with supervisors or managers, or with their colleagues in the CMHT. This is the case even when the CPN has decided to discharge a client.

With reference to the ideological and structural influences on psychiatric nursing practice, the CPNs do not have a professional discourse of their own and the content of their direct contact with clients is affected more by the medical model than any other perspective. The CPNs are influenced also by the uncertainty surrounding the commitment of the mental health disciplines (particularly that of psychology) to the organisational structure of the CMHT. Moreover, the CPNs' membership of the CMHT is undermined by their acceptance of self-referrals and referrals from general practitioners, without these clients first being reviewed collectively by the team. One other influence is the lack of supervision of the CPN's practice, either from within the discipline of community psychiatric nursing, or from other disciplines.

Relationships between the CPNs and their colleagues in the CMHT are reported to be characterised at times by interdisciplinary hostility. For example, conflict exists between members of the CMHT. This is focused in particular on the consultant psychiatrists' attempts to attain or retain dominance and the strategies that are adopted by the CPNs (and other members of the CMHT) to subvert these attempts.

Another aspect to the relationships within the CMHT is the perception of the consultant psychiatrists and the psychologists that they are the senior professional groups within the psychiatric service and nurses should provide a supportive role. Furthermore, although fogginess pervades the opinions of the members of the CMHT and the managers about just what the role of the CPN is, the key elements would appear to centre on the surveillance of the chronically mentally ill living in the community.

Chapter 7
Case Study:
Implications

The research problem addressed in the study discussed in the previous two chapters is concerned with the occupational position of community psychiatric nursing and, by implication, that of the whole of mental health nursing. Specifically, the study examined the claims of mental health nurses working in the community to have achieved (or to be in the process of achieving) 'clinical autonomy' and to explore the effects of becoming members of the CMHT on this autonomy.

Psychiatric nurses working in the community, by the nature of their work, operate much of the time beyond the 'gaze' of their line managers, or members of other professional groups. That is, CPNs and other community health workers (for example, health visitors, community midwives, district nurses) deliver their service away from any formal organisational setting – i.e. in the home of the service user. This is in direct contrast to the nurse working within an institution. As Nolan observes, referring to psychiatric nurses operating in the community, it is 'a very different experience for them entirely from working in mental hospitals' (1993, p137).

Furthermore, because they are not under the direct observation of managers and colleagues, community nurses have much more opportunity to influence the content and structure of their practice compared with nurses in institutions. In this study, the CPNs appeared to exercise a high degree of independence with respect to constructing the characteristics of their case loads. For example, they were able to determine who to discharge and when to discharge, what form of treatment to offer and how often to provide treatment. Moreover, the CPNs did not discuss regularly or meaningfully their clients with their colleagues and/or the referrers. Nor did they ask for, or receive, any substantial amount of organised supervision from either their colleagues or their managers.

The CPNs were able also to institute certain skulduggerous schemes to avoid their work being directed by other disciplines, particularly psychiatry. The potential for the profession of psychiatry to dominate CPNs was undermined further by the latter accepting referrals from general practitioners and self-referrals.

Autonomy by Default

The ability to work unhindered does not necessarily indicate the existence of authentic autonomy: 'Nightclub magicians and circus acrobats ... form autonomous occupations by virtue of their intensive specialisation ... Other occupations, like cab drivers or lighthouse keepers, are fairly autonomous because their work takes place in a mobile or physically segregated context that prevents others from observing and therefore evaluating and controlling, performance. In all these cases, we have autonomy by default' (Freidson, 1970b, pp136-7).

The 10 CPNs in this study, as in Freidson's example of the cab driver or lighthouse keeper, have gained a substantial level of autonomy over their work 'by default'. Unlike the autonomy afforded to such occupations as medicine, it is not legitimate. That is, the CPNs have not achieved their clinical autonomy through a successful campaign of occupational advancement, which has then been recognised and condoned by the state and the public. Nor do they occupy a position of dominance over other occupational groups within the CMHTs. They have autonomy because what they do in their practice has been left unobserved and unmanaged: 'CPNs make decisions about clinical situations that they have to deal with, often without consultation with anyone else, not necessarily by design but often because there isn't anybody else to consult with' (manager).

Lack of Rigour

CPN practice in the four teams studied in this research, far from exemplifying clinical autonomy, is depicted by a lack of rigour. The flawed work of the CPN is preserved by a 'collusive lethargy' on behalf of managers and colleagues. That is, neither those who have the bureaucratic authority to direct CPN practice, nor the 'senior' mental health professionals, endeavour to tackle a situation they are clearly unhappy with.

There are two crucial aspects to the unmanaged work of the CPNs. The first is the effect this has on the 'psychiatric careers' of their clients. The effect of nursing practice on users of the psychiatric services has been commented on by many authors (for example, Sharpe, 1982; Horrocks, 1985; Morrall, 1987a, 1987b; Simpson, 1988; Wooff et al., 1988; Wooff and Goldberg, 1988; Illing et al., 1990; Pollock, 1990). CPNs in this study regulated the form and trajectory of a client's clinical pathway using capricious and unsupervised decision-making processes about the length of time the client remains within the psychiatric system and what treatment is provided.

The second aspect is the way in which the CPNs act as pre-emptory gate keepers for the psychiatric services. Although the CPNs do not prevent an individual who has been referred to them from becoming a 'client' of the psychiatric system (because they accept all referrals on to their case loads), when they make the decision to attend general practitioners' surgeries they are, in effect, surveying prospective candidates for the social position of 'psychiatric patient'. Nurses, therefore, perform as 'psychiatric entrepreneurs'. They are involved actively in the categorisation and decategorisation of the population into the mad and not-mad, the reasonable and unreasonable, the normal and deviant.

There are two extreme examples of the CPNs' lack of rigour affecting directly the service users. First, on many occasions when CPNs went on holiday or were absent from work due to sickness (possibly for many weeks) no other practitioner contacted their clients. Second, CPNs appeared to discharge clients not only without any prior discussion with colleagues, supervisors or managers, but also without reference to any objective evaluation of the clients' fitness for discharge.

This latter practice has been condemned in the Ritchie Report (1994), which examined the circumstances that led to the murder of Jonathon Zito by Christopher Clunis. Clunis (diagnosed as a paranoid schizophrenic) killed Zito on a London Underground platform in December 1992. In April 1991, a CPN, who had been responsible for treating Clunis with injections of long-acting tranquillisers, had written to his general practitioner: 'At present there is very little I can do, so I am discharging him' (cited in the Ritchie Report, 1994, p36).

The implication is that this CPN (as with the nurses in the study reported here) informed the general practitioner of the decision to discharge after it had been determined to do so, rather than conducting a discussion about the appropriateness of this action before it was implemented.

It has become a central part of the remit of all inquiries into homicides committed by the mentally disordered to assess the competence of the relevant practitioners: 'Questioning of professional judgement ... lies at the heart of the inquiry process. Could the perpetrator's behaviour and the ultimate tragedy have been predicted or prevented? Should more care have been taken? Could mistakes have been avoided?' (Peay, 1996, p11).

The attention of the media has also been drawn to criticism of 'unrefined' practices by mental health workers: 'The body of a mentally ill man was found in his council flat weeks after he died and nearly six months after he was last seen by his community psychiatric nurse an inquest heard ... Malcolm McDuff ... had not had his monthly injection to control his schizophrenia since last December. Police found his body lying in an armchair last week, after being called in by neighbours who had not seen Mr McDuff for over a month' (Brindle, 1994c).

I am not suggesting that any of the 10 CPNs in this study were involved in misjudging such serious situations as those that have resulted in the deaths of innocent bystanders or their clients. Nor am I missing the point that no practitioner (whether a doctor, lecturer, lawyer or priest) is without imperfection in the delivery of her or his services. Furthermore, inquiries into homicides by the mentally ill, as well as the media, highlight the failings of practitioners other than nurses. It is my proposition, however, that the lax practices by psychiatric nurses identified in this study have the potential to lead to disaster, when and if, the 'right' circumstances transpire.

Lack of Resources

'One south London GP ... Dr Ratna ... like others in the field [i.e. GPs providing mental health care] ... fears that shortage of funding and a lack of rigour in the treatment of mental illness means that many individuals do not always get the most positive treatment' (Coward, 1992).

What is the connection between defective working procedures and the under-funding of state provision for the mentally ill?

The role of the CPN and expansion of the psychiatric nursing services are inextricably linked with the policy of care in the community for the mentally ill. The existence of community psychiatric nursing is a consequence of the decarceration of the mentally ill from mental hospitals. Government health policy has emphasised community care for the mentally ill since the 1960s (Jones, 1988; Means and Smith, 1994), although the debate about substituting institutional forms of treatment started as far back as the 1920s (Rogers and Pilgrim, 1996). In 1954, there were more than 150,000 patients living in mental hospitals (Barnes, 1990). This was the peak of psychiatric in-patient care. By 1991, there were only 63,000 in-patients (Hally, 1994). Many mental hospitals have now closed. Of the 130 mental hospitals in existence in 1960, it is predicted that only 22 will remain open by the end of the century (Health Committee, 1994).

Various explanations have been offered for the demise of institutional care (Miller and Rose, 1986; Pilgrim and Rogers, 1993). The development of pharmaceutical products in the 1950s, it is argued (particularly by the psychiatrists), has led to the possibility of people suffering from serious mental illnesses to be cared for in the community. It is suggested also that a reformist movement, propagated by both sociologists and medical practitioners, assisted the move towards community care:

'Erving Goffman published his sociological account of the effects of the "total institution" in stripping away the personality and identity of the inmate ... John Wing demonstrated that institutionalism ... was common to long stay inmates of even well-run mental hospitals ... the solution was not to reform the institution but to do away with it' (Miller and Rose, 1986, p54).

However, as we have noted in an earlier chapter, Scull (1983; 1984) has suggested that with the development of the welfare state, institutional segregation of the mentally ill (as a mechanism of social control) had become too expensive. Consequently, for Scull, the decline of the mental hospital and the rise of community care have been determined by economic considerations.

Indeed, the resourcing of care in the community remains a topical political issue. With reference to mental health, there continues to be the claim that there is insufficient funding for an effective community care policy. For example, in the House of Commons Health Committee Report (Health Committee, 1994) a case is presented for the government to divert resources into inner-city areas. It is suggested in this report that a permanent Inter-departmental National Advisory Group on Mental Health is set up to oversee policy relating to care in the community to ensure that 'adequate resources are made available for its recommendations' (pxxiv).

The Audit Commission (1994) reports that although mental hospitals have closed, 92 still remain open. The commission observes that a serious under-resourcing of community care is occurring because most of the funding for adult mental health care in England and Wales (£1.8 billion a year) is spent on hospitals.

Although it recognises that London can be regarded as an extreme case because of its high levels of unemployment, social isolation, homelessness and large ethnic and refugee populations, the King's Fund report into the condition of the capital's hospital and community mental health provision concludes that 'mental health services in London are substantially under-funded' (Johnson et al., 1997, p362).

Alarmingly, the report states that the way in which the present services are operating is not sustainable. Despite the need for extra resources, the report comments that some London boroughs are proposing to reduce funding for mental health services.

The situation in other western countries would appear not to be too dissimilar, as is indicated in the following newspaper commentaries from New Zealand:

'Health Minister Jenny Shipley says she will investigate how a psychiatric patient gave birth to a baby on a Waitangarua street after her release from Porirua Hospital. The woman was found by a taxi driver ... He said that her English was not good ... The incident has renewed concerns about the resourcing of mental health services' (Vasil, 1995).

'Police in Palmerston North are "sick and tired" of being the response unit at the bottom of the cliff for mentally ill people who have not been adequately cared for by the health system. Police association spokesman Ian Sutherland said today it was obvious the Government was providing inadequate resources to handle the problem' (staff reporters, 1995).

Scull's view is that the consequence of under-resourcing community care is the creation of a 'nightmare existence' (1984, p2) for discharged mentally ill people. They have become, argues Scull, neglected and homeless.

However, Scull's analysis of the causes and process of decarcerating the mentally ill into the community has many deficiencies, a number of which I have described already. One further and fundamental problem with Scull's approach is that although he does accept that the impact of decarceration in Britain has been less severe than in the United States, very few homeless people in this country are former psychiatric inpatients (Audit Commission, 1994). But the plight of mentally ill people living in the community in this country, even if they have not been 'decarcerated' from a hospital, is still stark:

'Surveys have shown that the proportions of mentally disturbed people in single homeless hostel populations have grown ... In the 1980s most surveys found that 30-40% had overt psychiatric disorder ... The number of destitute people with serious mental disorder now living more or less permanently in this way is reckoned to be 60-90,000' (Murphy, 1991, p211).

However, unlike Pollock, who concluded that the decisions of the CPNs in her study were 'strongly influenced by the lack of resources' (1989, p195), a lack of rigour is not necessarily occurring in the teams examined in the research study I conducted because of the unavailability of appropriate funding. A shortage of staff and/or an over-subscription of numbers of clients did not seem to be a major cause of concern for any of the informants. This was perceived also to be the case in the report into the killing of occupational therapist Georgina Robinson by a psychiatric patient: 'None of the professionals [including CPNs] complained to us of overwork' (Blom-Cooper et al., 1996, p166).

Again, I do not wish to suggest that there was any wilful dereliction of duty by the practitioners involved in this research. Indeed, even Lucy Johnson, an inveterate critic of the psychiatric system, accepts that 'the great majority of psychiatric staff are dedicated and hard-working people with a genuine wish to help the patients they are paid to care for' (Johnstone, 1989, p153). As Peay notes, the inquiries into mental health services perceived to have failed to protect the public from the dangerously ill, have the advantage of hindsight and are subject to the intense questioning of an inquiry committee. Under these conditions, Peay asks the rhetorical question: 'Which of us would be likely to be found completely without fault?' (Peay, 1996, p11).

Indeed, the same observation could be made with respect to the 'intense' research methods of this study. That is, during many hours of interviewing, an informant is much more likely to expose her or his imperfections than prove to be faultless.

However, what I argue is that the practice of the psychiatric nurses is affected detrimentally where supervision, leadership, descriptions of roles, responsibilities and lines of authority, are not delineated. This is an issue that concerns the overall organisation and future direction of mental health nursing and the psychiatric services. Any accusation of role-deviation or culpability on the part of the individual CPN is inappropriate as neither the ideal typification of role performance, nor perceived role expectations, are expressed coherently and systematically by the health service managers. Conversely, it could be argued that if role-deviancy exists among the CPNs then it is propagated by ineffective management due to, for example, inadequate and non-mandatory supervisory systems.

Furthermore, although Scull's theory of economic determinism in relation to the decarceration of the mentally ill is weak, his economic perspective does raise the questions of why the CPNs have *'de facto* autonomy' and why there is a 'lack of rigour'. That is, Scull's analysis may lead to the suspicion that it is financially expedient for both the state and National Health Service managers to avoid insisting that community care services are made more effective (through, for example, the stringent supervision of CPN practice) because of the consequent expense. Moreover, if mental health nurses venture into largely uncharted territory by working with the homeless, as is advocated implicitly by the Audit Commission (1994) and explicitly by the Mental Health Nursing Review team (DoH, 1994b), there may be tremendous, and therefore prohibitive, cost implications. There is, therefore, every temptation for the government to ignore the 'lack of rigour – cost of rigour' equation.

Reconstructing Practice

'CPNs may be described as the "artful dodgers" of the mental health world. They have expanded only by stealing roles previously belonging to other occupations without quite knowing what to do when they have them' (Sheppard, 1991, p161).

What then is the way forward for CPNs and mental health nursing overall? The criticisms of many of the CPNs' colleagues in the CMHTs examined in this study concur with the recommendation of the Audit Commission (1994) that psychiatric nurses should change their focus of attention from the 'worried well' to treating people with serious mental illness. This is also the stated position of the mental health nursing review team: 'Mental health nurses should focus on people who have serious or enduring mental illness' (DoH, 1994b, p28).

It would appear also that the Labour Party, while accepting that there is a need for further training, is fully in support of mental health nurses concentrating on working with 'severe' illness: 'These changes [i.e. Labour Party Policy on mental health] will allow CPNs to use their specific skills to focus on the care of patients with the greatest need. But if CPNs are to be the prime providers of care programmes for people with the most severe mental health problems, then new training policies are required' (Milburn, 1996, p9).

In the Ritchie Report, people with a 'serious' mental distress are identified as suffering from psychotic illnesses such as 'schizophrenia, schizo-affective disorder, paranoid psychosis, manic-depression or a major depression' (1994, pvii). The trend, however, has been for CPNs to move more and more away from working with this group of clients (Brooker and Butterworth, 1991). In this study, only a minority (16%; n = 42) of the new clients (n = 252) were described as suffering from delusions and/or hallucinations. Moreover, as White (1993) has reported from a comprehensive survey of CPNs in England, 25% of CPNs do not have one client on their case loads with the diagnosis of schizophrenia.

There is, however, much debate about definitions of 'serious' mental illness. For example, Barker and Jackson (1997) argue there is a series of 'new epidemics' that should not be overlooked because numerically these are now more significant than many psychotic illnesses. These new epidemics are seen to be: depression in old age, among children and adolescents and a rising incidence in men; eating disorders; personality disorder; self-mutilation and suicide; mental distress as a direct result of sexual abuse in childhood and from contracting dementia, HIV and AIDS.

Barker and Jackson claim that the consequence of expressly targeting long-term disorder is to direct psychiatric nursing towards the specialist mental health services: 'Mental health nursing is being refocused on the tertiary support of a declining population of people with a chronic mental illness – a classic case of closing the stable door after the horse has bolted' (Barker and Jackson, 1997, p41).

On the other hand, Barker and Jackson argue for the psychiatric nurse to ally with the primary services to help deal with the new epidemics. They point out that the health agenda of the United Kingdom is converging on primary care. For them, the task of nursing, therefore, should be to offer a service across the range of established mental disorder and to the rising population of people experiencing 'problems with living' in a world full of complexity and ill-defined expectations.

But to a considerable extent, Barker and Jackson's categories overlap with those listed in the Ritchie Report (1994). It is, therefore, somewhat ingenuous of these authors to attempt to make a distinction between, for example, a depressive illness occurring at a particular age and 'depression' as an overarching diagnostic rubric that covers all ages. Moreover, Barker and Jackson appear to ignore the possibility of some or all of the new epidemics being recognised as 'serious' mental disorders alongside the traditional psychoses and for a readjusted catalogue of illnesses to be treated by the specialist psychiatric services.

Furthermore, there continues to be pressure on psychiatric nurses to realign with consultant psychiatrists and the biomedical model. As I have argued earlier, both the profession of medicine and the biomedical model have not been removed from their powerful influence in the health care arena. The medical profession (underpinned by biomedicine), far from being challenged by such factors as alternative therapy and managerialism, is accommodating these threats and consolidating, if not improving, its occupational location. For example, the data from this study indicate that quasi-professional groups such as mental health nursing remain susceptible to dominance from psychiatry. Moreover, the therapies in psychiatry that do not belong to the category of biomedicine are themselves being criticised for their ineffectiveness and the non-professional behaviour of those that use them (Masson, 1990; Illman, 1993; Spinelli, 1994). With particular reference to CPNs, Gournay (1994) states: 'In recent years, CPNs have increasingly begun to use a wide range of therapeutic techniques. However, few ... are supported by any research-based literature' (p40).

A strengthened alliance with the medical profession for mental health nurses, however, does not preclude involvement with other therapeutic approaches (Brooker and Butterworth, 1993; Owen, 1994). Indeed, medicine does not limit itself to physical explanations and treatments. But, as Gournay (1990) suggests, advances in such areas as molecular genetics may result in an inevitable resurgence in the status of biomedicine and the power of medical practitioners in the decision-making process. Therefore, in coming once again under the direct influence of psychiatry, mental health nursing is more likely to survive as a distinct discipline. That is, linking with medical practitioners could be the most appropriate occupational strategy for a discipline that appears to have lost the opportunity to become a profession because it has failed to produce a self-regulated area of practice and ideology of its own and whose members might otherwise become a 'dying breed' (McIntegart, 1990).

Under the auspices of the consultant psychiatrist, the main function of the CPN may become one that consists of administering and observing the effects of medication, and 'surveillance'. The latter would entail the monitoring of the mental state of clients (e.g. alert for early signs of deterioration) and 'risk assessment'. It would also involve the psychiatric nurses participating actively in the implementation of supervision registers (NHS Management Executive, 1994) and the 1995 Mental

Health (Patients in the Community) Act. Such legislation should: 'Establish the CPN in a key role in relation to clients with long-term difficulties. It is time for CPNs to embrace this group' (Hally, 1994, p11).

There could, therefore, be an increase in the performance of the psychiatric nurse as an agent of social control.

If psychiatric nurses were to embrace the law in this way and accentuate their role as overseers of the mad, they could become complicit in what Bean (1993) has described as an 'Orwellian nightmare'. The negative effect of assisting in the maintenance of order in society is to fortify social configurations and centres of authority which create disadvantage, inequalities and scapegoating – all of which has a pernicious and disempowering effect on the mentally ill (Morrall, 1996).

But the identification of structures in society that worsen the predicament of the mentally ill should not deflect attempts to prevent the increasing incidence of apparent neglect by those charged with delivering psychiatric services (Sims, 1993; Brindle, 1994d; O'Connor, 1994; Ritchie, 1994). For example, the National Schizophrenic Fellowship (1992) has claimed that, of the 4000 people discharged from mental hospitals over a period of one year, 100 were associated with cases of suicide or murder. Boyd (1994), while recognising the danger of over-stating the significance of the role of the mentally ill in the rising homicide rate, concedes that during an 18 month period, 34 killings were committed by people who had been treated previously for mental illness. Consequently, it could be argued that by adopting this surveillance role, the occupational identity of mental health nurses will be more secure and, at the same time, they would be serving the best interests of the mentally ill: 'Maybe the pendulum swung too far: "freedom" can be a euphemism for neglect and neglect can be as cruel as oppression' (Porter, 1993).

Summary

The ramifications of the results from the case study of the work of psychiatric nurses working in the community raise issues that perhaps many both within and without the discipline would rather see remain dormant. If the results of further research were to corroborate those from this study, then the question of 'what should be the objective of mental health nursing' requires considerable attention. Linked to this question and in need of equal solicitude, but perhaps greater assiduity and openness, are the serious issues of mental health nurses' clinical competence and their social assignment to uphold order.

Conclusion

The conclusion from the research study described in the previous three chapters is that, when community psychiatric nurses gain clinical independence and thereby appear to have achieved a key element of professionalism, it is only *de facto* (not *de jure*) autonomy. The corollary of this is that, if psychiatric nurses operating in the community do not possess authentic clinical freedom, then those who work within the various institutions of psychiatry are constrained even further in their ability to become professionalised.

Furthermore, the evidence from the literature on professionalism compounds the conclusions from the study. That is, the theories on professions indicate that the medical profession continues to dominate nursing and that the domination of mental health nursing by psychiatry results in the former being tied to the 'social control' function of the latter.

Moreover, psychiatric nursing has to contend with two indomitable strands to the mental health industry's *Zeitgeist*. First, psychiatric nurses are being propelled towards concentrating their skills on the care of the long-term and seriously mentally ill. Second, they are confronted by a profession of psychiatric medicine rejuvenated by interminable biomedical discoveries, which eulogises over the scientific merits of the 'random controlled trial' while at the same time engulfing successfully all other epistemological contenders. Inevitably, any 'way forward' for nurses in the field of mental health must accommodate these powerful components of the present-day psychiatric services.

Psychiatric nursing cooperates thoroughly in the enforcement of control in society. Nurses regulate behaviour on behalf of the state either indirectly (i.e. through the auspices of psychiatric medicine) or directly by their own actions. This is most obvious when the mental health nurse gains employment in the locked world of forensic psychiatry, whether this be in the special hospitals, medium secure units, or 'intensive care wards'.

However, the social control element of the psychiatric nurse's actions is largely surreptitious and insidious and therefore all the more effective in controlling the mentally ill. For example, when purporting to operate from a humanistic and user-centred perspective (Dexter and Wash, 1986) , as 'advocate' for their clients (Duxbury, 1996), intervening as part of a 'court diversion scheme' (DOH/HO, 1992; Maclean, 1995), or 'police liaison nurse' (Tendler, 1995), they have the appearance of acting as subversives against the power of psychiatry and the state. However, ultimately, they are sanctioning and propagating the processes of dividing the population into the insane and sane, or in the case of their role in court diversion schemes and police liaison, separating the 'mad' from the 'bad'.

In the final analysis, the psychiatric nurse's role is at best one of apologist for the more obvious omnipotent features of psychiatry and the state. The primordial function of the psychiatric nurse in society is revealed as one of social control, however, when she or he engages the powers and directives of the law to: prevent 'informal' patients from leaving the psychiatric hospital; maintain supervision registers; force the non-compliant to take medication; apply physical restraints on 'aggressive' in-patients.

Policing the Mad

'We have homicides occurring because nobody will take ultimate responsibility for those people who are a risk to themselves and others' (Jane Zito in Cooper, 1995).

Only a small number of people labelled mentally ill are either aggressive to others or to themselves. People diagnosed schizophrenic are much more likely to commit suicide than homicide (Boyd, 1996). The number of homicides carried out by 'normal' people is growing, whereas the homicide rate among the mentally ill is relatively static. Moreover, the media are accused of exaggerating, if not completely fictionalising, the danger from mentally ill people and of scapegoating a vulnerable social group: 'There are many misconceptions about psychiatric patients. Surveys consistently show that the general public believe they are unpredictable, potentially dangerous and likely to commit violent and sexual crimes ... This damaging and inaccurate picture is heavily reinforced by the media, where headlines like "Ex-mental patient sought by police" and "Mad axeman kills two" are never balanced by more positive reports ("Ex-mental patient elected mayor", or 'Former patient rescues drowning girl")' (Johnstone, 1989, p20).

Since 1994, I have collected and analysed data from both broadsheet and tabloid newspaper reports and from the publications of the scores of public, government and health authority inquiries, about homicides committed by the mentally ill in the United Kingdom. The following list contains only a sample of the homicides registered in these sources. The terminology used here (for example, with reference to the diagnosis of the culprit, or the form of identity given to the victim) has been extracted from the original source:

Andrew Robinson: diagnosed as a paranoid schizophrenic, killed an occupational therapist.

John Rous: diagnosed as a schizophrenic, killed a residential care worker.

Robert Napper: diagnosed as a psychopath, killed and mutilated a woman and suffocated her four-year-old daughter.

Alan Boland: a discharged mental patient, confessed to killing his mother and committed suicide while on remand in prison.

Michael Buchanan: killed a former policeman two weeks after his discharge from a mental hospital.

Lukewarm Luke (Michael Folkes): a mental patient with a history of violence and rape, killed his girlfriend by stabbing her 70 times.

Wayne Hutchinson: diagnosed as a paranoid schizophrenic, killed two people and injured three others.

Paul Medley: diagnosed as a paranoid schizophrenic, killed a pensioner.

Jason Mitchell: diagnosed as a paranoid schizophrenic, killed his mother and two other people.

Paul Gordon: a former psychiatric patient, killed an elderly man.

Christopher Farrage: diagnosed as a paranoid schizophrenic, killed his mother with a weight-lifting barbell and by repeated stabbing.

Stephen Wilkinson: described as a paranoid schizophrenic, killed a schoolgirl during a maths lesson.

Gerald O'Dowd: diagnosed as a paranoid schizophrenic, killed his wife by stabbing her through the heart and was convicted of manslaughter on the grounds of diminished responsibility.

Stephen Laudat: diagnosed as a schizophrenic, stabbed to death a fellow patient whom he believed to be Ronnie Kray.

Robert Viner: diagnosed as a schizophrenic, found dead after apparently killing his mother.

Patrick Alesworth: described as suffering from mental illness for more than 30 years, killed his daughter with a hammer and committed suicide in the grounds of the psychiatric hospital he had been sent to after being convicted of manslaughter by reason of diminished responsibility.

Martin Mursell: diagnosed as a paranoid schizophrenic, killed his step-father and stabbed his mother.

Nilesh Gadher: diagnosed as a paranoid schizophrenic, killed a woman by driving his car at her in a car park.

Anthony Smith: diagnosed as a paranoid schizophrenic, killed his mother and half-brother.

Celia Beckett: described as suffering from severe personality problems, killed one of her daughters and poisoned another.

Darren Carr: diagnosed as suffering from a psychopathic disorder, killed a mother and her two children by setting fire to the house he shared with them.

Claire Bosley: described in police psychiatric evidence as suffering from paranoid depression, killed her husband and committed suicide while on remand in prison.

Susan Hearman: diagnosed as having a severe personality disorder, killed a
mother and her two daughters by setting fire to the home she shared with
them and was convicted of manslaughter on the grounds of diminished
responsibility.

It is well understood that the media 'edit' and skew the messages they
compose by focusing on particular parts of a story and through the use
of value-laden adjectives and images (Ramon, 1996). There are
undoubtedly interpretative processes in the 'construction' of the above
events that need to be acknowledged. For example, in some of the
cases cited the offender is labelled 'mentally ill' only after she or he has
entered the judicial system. That is, the categorisation of murderous
behaviour as 'insanity' may be one of political or legal convenience
intended to explain the inexplicable (Prins, 1995), rather than an accurate representation of those considered to be the 'norm' of the mad
population.

However, these incidents are 'real' in the sense that people have
died and others have been incarcerated. Moreover, whether the number of homicides by the mentally ill pales into insignificance when compared with the number of 'normal' murders is beside the point.
Subsequent to the death of Jonathan Zito at the hands of Christopher
Clunis in 1992, scores of people have been killed, many hundreds more
have been left bereaved and still more are in dread of what could happen: 'Every time they hear that a mental patient has killed or injured
someone, Bill and Diana ... feel a spasm of fear. Their 23-year-old son
... was diagnosed as schizophrenic four years ago. In his stormiest
phases, he becomes violent and browbeats his parents for money. He
has threatened to kill himself, kill them, burn the house down. What
must they do, his parents ask – and more terrifyingly, what must *he* do
– in order to get the treatment his condition so obviously requires?'
(Grice, 1996).

This problem must not be ignored simply because the bigger issue
of crime by 'normal' people is awaiting resolution. The perceived
dangerousness of the mentally ill, even if it is 'amplified' by the
media, does warrant society's intervention to safeguard potential victims and perpetrators:

'The social order is a sacred right which is the basis of all other rights ... The
problem is to find a form of association which will defend and protect with
the whole common force the person and goods of each associate and in
which each, while uniting himself with all, may still obey himself alone, and
remain as free as before' (Jean-Jacques Rousseau, Du Contrat Social, 1762).

At this time, when violence by mentally ill people is receiving so
much public and political attention, it may be propitious, therefore, for
psychiatric nursing to seize a 'market opportunity', augmenting and
strengthening their social control function. That is, a case can be made

for psychiatric nurses to realise and actuate the primary reason for their existence, expanding their role as legitimate agents of social control, thereby fostering social stability as well as protecting the mentally ill from abuse and neglect. Under the guidance of psychiatrists and the burgeoning medical model, this role could be broadened, publicised and developed as an occupational strategy to replace that of professionalism.

Part of this strategy must entail psychiatric nurses, whether they are working in hospitals or the community, devoting most of their practice to dealing with people suffering from serious mental illness. Included within the notion of 'serious' illness would be the traditional psychotic illnesses, as well as many of what Barker and Jackson (1997) have discerned as the 'new epidemics' of mental disorder. Although the consequence of enlarging the category of 'serious' mental illness to embrace those suffering from these new epidemics would be to 'psychiatrise' yet more of the populace, the benefit to psychiatric nursing would be an expansion of its therapeutic territory.

The main tasks of the psychiatric nurse in these circumstances would be to: accumulate knowledge about psychopharmacology and other biomedical treatments being developed in psychiatry; administer and review the effects of medication; monitor the mental state of clients; report signs of mental deterioration; assess risk of aggression, suicide and homicide; be instrumental in the implementation of the 'supervision' and 'treatment' aspects of recent mental health legislation; operate 'crisis' facilities designed to provide prompt and 24 hour assistance to the mentally ill and their families caught in 'violent' situations.

Psychiatric Perestroika

> 'There are some 250 million severely mentally ill people in the world ... the treatment of the mentally ill should be a major concern' (Cohen, 1988, p7).

It is possible for a proportion of the fraternity of psychiatric nurses to contemplate a very different occupational thrust. A radical stance could be forged, with international cooperation, from the conviction that the mentally ill are a severely disadvantaged group in many different societies.

Throughout the world, the mad are exposed to the 'low level' defilement and molestation that accompanies a life at the bottom of the social pile. In such diverse countries as the United States of America, Hungary, Japan, Egypt, India, Greece, Israel and the United Kingdom, they are stigmatised, taunted and ill-treated by neighbours, family and at times by the very 'professionals' who have been given the responsibility for their care (Cohen, 1988; Borger, 1994; Ramon, 1996).

Borger describes the situation in Bulgaria. Here the all-encompassing diagnostic stamp of 'oligophrenia' is used to channel children as young as three, who are suffering from extremely disparate types of psychiatric difficulties (e.g. learning disabilities; epilepsy; schizophrenia), into grossly inadequate institutional care. Referring to one such residence, Borger writes about his own observations: 'The inmates ... are worse off than prisoners. As mental patients, they have fewer rights. In the main building, about 30 patients are crammed into one dark, stinking room, huddled in their blankets around a wood stove, shouting, muttering and squabbling. They defecate and urinate on the concrete floor. Most faces bear the scabs of past fights' (Borger, 1994).

In Britain, the voluntary mental health organisation, MIND, surveyed a self-selected sample (n = 778) of its own membership and uncovered a wide range of harassment (Brindle, 1996). This included: being hit by stones and eggs; receiving offensive mail; having excrement, used condoms and burning matches through letter boxes; and suffering from intimidation in the workplace. More than 200 of the informants reported that they had also been forced to move house because of the persecution they had experienced from the 'community' in which they lived.

The mad, because they are perceived to endanger the edifices of authority, are also prone to 'high level' desecration by the socially powerful: 'The history of madness is the history of power. It requires power to control it. Threatening the normal structures of authority, insanity is engaged in an endless dialogue ... about power' (Porter, 1987, p39).

Power is distributed unequally on the basis of such social structures as gender, age, material wealth, class, employment/occupational status and ethnicity (Morrall, 1995c). The mad are in 'double jeopardy' because of the contempt society associates with their condition and the stigma attributed to their low social placement caused by, for example, poverty, homelessness or unemployment.

In the past, an individual regarded as mad was segregated from society to thwart the destabilising effect of her or his deviant *persona*. Nowadays, she or he may be found within society, but is marginalised and therefore retains an identity of *persona non grata*.

Detachment from mainstream society means that social deprivation is common among the mentally ill (Audit Commission, 1994; Johnson et al., 1997). Furthermore, the socially contaminated and economically non-viable can be excluded readily from health care systems available to the remaining population. For example, the Association of Community Health Councils for England and Wales reported on a survey of more than 200 community health councils (Brindle, 1994b). In one year, general practitioners were found to have removed from their lists approximately 30,000 patients. Many of these patients were mentally disordered, whose treatment, along with other chronically sick people and the elderly, is expensive and time-consuming.

Incongruously, however, there is an ongoing campaign to include the opinions of the mentally ill in the evaluation of the quality of the psychiatric services. This movement has been endorsed by a wide range of policy-making organisations (Audit Commission, 1994; DoH, 1994b; Health Committee, 1994; Blom-Cooper et al., 1995; ENB, 1996; McAndrew, 1996; Johnson et al., 1997). Interest in the empowerment of the 'citizen' in general was stimulated by the approach of the World Health Organisation to health promotion, which commenced in the 1980s (Gibson, 1991). This promoted the principle of 'self-help', whereby individuals would be encouraged to take control of their own lives rather than rely completely on the state for health and welfare provision.

Allowing the mentally ill to submit their views about the treatment they receive does not, however, negate the disempowering effects of the structural parameters and imperatives that maintain their low social status. Nor does is it alleviate the cumulative effect of a social existence characterised by demeaning interpersonal relationships. Enabling the mentally ill to participate in the organisation of their care and treatment is nothing more than tokenism, unless the social, political, economic and cultural conditions that shape disadvantage are incorporated into a programme of change.

The discipline of clinical sociology (Rebach and Bruhn, 1991; Blane, 1993) could provide a dynamic and politically informed foundation to the therapeutic actions of some mental health nurses (Morrall, 1996). The theories of sociology, applied to the clinical arena, can demystify the structural and interpersonal conditions that manipulate power and indicate ways in which the individual and society can progress: 'The work of clinical sociology has the goal of planned positive social change on a case-by-case basis. The clinical sociologist recognises that human problems are rooted in social life' (Rebach and Bruhn, 1991, p14).

Armed with the theory and skills emanating from clinical sociology and sustained by the morally justified intention of increasing the empowerment of their clients and curbing the intemperate conduct of a rampant and hegemonic medical enterprise, the psychiatric nurse can apply herself or himself to helping the mentally ill gain humane living conditions, employment and fight personal and structural discrimination.

What I am envisaging is the formulation of a trans-national cadre of like-minded, self-appointed agents of social change rather than social control. Many psychiatric nurses may find the prospect of exploiting a 'niche market' and forming the 'new anti-psychiatry' a seductive occupational and philosophical alternative to that of either professionalism or 'policing the mad'.

Appendix 1

Diary–interview Schedule

1. CPN no.   [ ][ ]
2. Centre number: [ ]
Date research commenced:
Date research completed:

Community psychiatric nurse profile

3. Age:
    - (1) 20–29 years   [ ]
    - (2) 30–39 years   [ ]
    - (3) 40–49 years   [ ]
    - (4) 50–59 years   [ ]   [ ]
    - (5) 60 + years   [ ]

4. Gender:
    - (1) Female   [ ]   [ ]
    - (2) Male   [ ]

5. Ethnicity:
    - (1) Caucasian/White   [ ]
    - (2) Afro-Caribbean   [ ]
    - (3) Asian   [ ]   [ ]
    - (4) Oriental   [ ]
    - (5) Other   [ ]

Qualifications completed/being undertaken (excluding RMN):

6. RGN   [ ]
7. RNMH   [ ]
8. RSCN   [ ]

9. SEN   [ ]
10. EN (M)   [ ]
11. CPN Cert./Diploma ENB 810   [ ]
12. CPN Cert./Diploma ENB 811   [ ]
13. Counselling Cert./Diploma   [ ]
14. Psychotherapy Cert./Diploma   [ ]
15. Behaviour Therapy Cert./Dip   [ ]
16. Dip. in Nursing (old regs.)   [ ]
17. Dip. in Nursing (new regs.)   [ ]
18. Degree (e.g. BSc/BA/BEd/MA)   [ ]
19. Other   [ ]

Notes:

20. Date RMN obtained:
      (1) Before 1980   [ ]
      (2) 1980-1985   [ ]   [ ]
      (3) 1986 or later   [ ]

21. Trained on the '1982' syllabus?   [ ]

22. Present employment grade:
      (1) E   [ ]
      (2) F   [ ]   [ ]
      (3) G   [ ]
      (4) H   [ ]

23. Length of time spent as a CPN:
      (1) Under 1 year   [ ]
      (2) One year or more but less than two   [ ]
      (3) Two years or more but less than three   [ ]   [ ]
      (4) Three years or more but less than four [ ]
      (5) Five years or more   [ ]

Notes:

Team membership:

24. Member of a psychiatric MDT   [ ]
25. Member of a CMHT   [ ]
26. Member of a PHCT   [ ]
27. Other   [ ]

Notes:

28. Size of case-load in total:
      (1) Below 10   [ ]
      (2) Between 10 and 20   [ ]
      (3) Between 21 and 30   [ ]   [ ]
      (4) Between 31 and 40   [ ]
      (5) 41 and above   [ ]

Referral sources:

29. Any referral source
    (including all of those below)   [ ]
30. Consultant psychiatrist   [ ]
31. Any member of the psychiatric medical team   [ ]
32. GPs   [ ]
33. Any medical practitioner   [ ]
34. Social workers/Social services   [ ]
35. Psychologists   [ ]
36. CPNs   [ ]
37. Any member of the MDT   [ ]
38. Any member of the PHCT   [ ]
39. Any member of the CMHT   [ ]
40. Team leader   [ ]
41. Supervisor   [ ]
42. Manager   [ ]
43. Clients (self-referrals)   [ ]
44. Voluntary agencies   [ ]
45. Other   [ ]

Notes:

Operational site(s):

46. Grounds of psychiatric hospital   [ ]
47. CMHC/Resource centre   [ ]
48. GP surgery   [ ]
49. DGH   [ ]
50. Other   [ ]

Notes:

Clinical supervision:

51. CPN receives formal clinical supervision   [ ]
52. CPN receives informal clinical supervision   [ ]

Notes:

Referral profile

1. CPN no.   [ ] [ ]
2. Team no.   [ ]
53. Referral no.   [ ] [ ]
54. Week no. (1–15)   [ ] [ ]
55. Immediate referral source:
     (1) Consultant psychiatrist   [ ]
     (2) Other member of the psychiatric
     medical team   [ ]
     (3) GP   [ ]
     (4) Medical practitioner other than above   [ ]
     (5) Social worker   [ ]
     (6) Psychologist   [ ]
     (7) CPN   [ ]
     (8) MDT   [ ]
     (9) PHCT   [ ] [ ] [ ]
     (10) CMHT   [ ]
     (11) District nurse   [ ]
     (12) Health visitor   [ ]
     (13) Team leader   [ ]
     (14) Supervisor   [ ]
     (15) Manager   [ ]
     (16) Self-referred   [ ]
     (17) Voluntary agency   [ ]
     (18) Other   [ ]

Notes:

56. Original referral source:
     (1) Same as immediate referral source   [ ]
     (2) Consultant psychiatrist   [ ]
     (3) Other member of the psychiatric
        medical team   [ ]
     (4) GP   [ ]
     (5) Medical practitioner other than above   [ ]
     (6) Social worker   [ ]
     (7) Psychologist   [ ]
     (8) CPN   [ ]
     (9) MDT   [ ] [ ] [ ]
     (10) PHCT   [ ]
     (11) CMHT   [ ]
     (12) District nurse   [ ]
     (13) Health visitor   [ ]
     (14) Team leader   [ ]
     (15) Supervisor   [ ]

(16) Manager   [ ]
(17) Self-referred   [ ]
(18) Voluntary agency   [ ]
(19) Other   [ ]

Notes:

57. Age:
    (1) Below 20 years   [ ]
    (2) 20–29 years   [ ]
    (3) 30–39 years   [ ] [ ]
    (4) 40–49 years   [ ]
    (5) 50–59 years   [ ]
    (6) 60+   [ ]

58. Gender:
    (1) Female   [ ] [ ]
    (2) Male   [ ]

59. Ethnicity:
    (1) Caucasian/White   [ ]
    (2) Afro-Caribbean   [ ]
    (3) Asian   [ ] [ ]
    (4) Oriental   [ ]
    (5) Other   [ ]

60. Marital status:
    (1) Single   [ ]
    (2) Married   [ ]
    (3) Separated   [ ]
    (4) Divorced   [ ] [ ]
    (5) Cohabiting   [ ]
    (6) Widowed   [ ]
    (7) Other   [ ]

61. Employment status:
    (1) Full-time Reg. Gen. Category {i}   [ ]
    (2)   "   {ii}   [ ]
    (3)   "   {iii}   [ ]
    (4)   "   {iv}   [ ]
    (5)   "   {v}   [ ]
    (6) Part-time   [ ] [ ] [ ]
    (7) Full-time housewife/husband   [ ]
    (8) Unemployed   [ ]
    (9) Full-time student   [ ]
    (10) Other (e.g. retired)   [ ]

Notes:

62. Indication of referrer's expectations: (ref. Barratt, 1989)
    (1) Assessment   [ ]

        (2) Counselling   [ ]
        (3) Giving medication   [ ]
        (4) Other physical care   [ ]
        (5) Advising   [ ]
        (6) Education   [ ] [ ] [ ]
        (7) Specialist therapy   [ ]
        (8) Reassurance/Support   [ ]
        (9) Monitoring   [ ]
        (10) Evaluating   [ ]
        (11) Unspecified   [ ]
        (12) Other   [ ]

Notes:

Client's psychiatric history:

63. Previous in-patient care   [ ]
64. Previous out-patient care   [ ]
65. Previously treated by GP for a/this
    'psychiatric' problem   [ ]
66. Previous CPN involvement   [ ]
67. No known previous psychiatric history   [ ]

Notes:

68. Major presenting symptom/behaviour:
        (1) Anxiety   [ ]
        (2) Depression   [ ]
        (3) Phobia   [ ]
        (4) Delusions   [ ]
        (5) Hallucinations   [ ]
        (6) Delusions and hallucinations   [ ]
        (7) Confusion   [ ]
        (8) Overactivity (hypomania/mania)   [ ] [ ] [ ]
        (9) Aggression   [ ]
        (10) Self-harm (actual)   [ ]
        (11) Self-harm (implied)   [ ]
        (12) Drug/alcohol addiction   [ ]
        (13) 'Problems with living'   [ ]
        (14) Sexual problems   [ ]
        (15) Over eating/Under eating   [ ]
        (16) Other   [ ]

Notes:

69. Key worker attached to client:
    (1) Above-named CPN   [ ]
    (2) Other CPN   [ ]
    (3) Other MDT member (not a CPN)   [ ]
    (4) Other CMHT member (not a CPN)   [ ] [ ]
    (5) Other PHCT member (not a CPN)   [ ]
    (6) No key worker identified   [ ]
    (7) Above CPN with other colleague   [ ]

Notes:

70. Length of time monitored (by researcher)
    (1) One week only   [ ]
    (2) Two to four weeks   [ ]
    (3) Five to seven weeks   [ ] [ ]
    (4) Eight to ten weeks   [ ]
    (5) Eleven or more weeks   [ ]
71. Client outcome:
    (1) Care continued   [ ]
    (2) Re-referred to other MH professional   [ ] [ ]
    (3) Discharged   [ ]
    (4) Other   [ ]

Notes:

72. Why did you accept this particular referral?
    [Probes: Was it delegated to you? If so by whom?
    Did it follow from negotiations with colleagues? If so, who with?
    Did you accept it because you felt that you had the
    appropriate skills?   [ ] [ ]
    Do you accept all referrals?
    What would have happened if you hadn't accepted this referral?]
      (1) Arbitrary. ('Because I answered the phone'; 'I had space on
           my case-load'; 'Nobody else available')
      (2) Interesting. ('I found this client's details interesting')
      (3) Speciality. ('My skills appear to meet the client's needs')
      (4) Delegation/Request. ('I was asked specifically to deal with
           this client' [e.g. by GP]; 'I was delegated this client' [e.g. by
           manager/consultant/supervisor/superior]; 'I was asked to
           see the client by a colleague')
      (5) Appropriate. ('Because the referral seemed appropriate';
           'It was urgent')
      (6) CMHT. (The team generally)
      (7) Objective. (The use of an agreed upon assessment format)

(8) Unspecified
(9) Other
(10) Re-referral (CPN had previously dealt with client)

CPN–referral 'action' probe sheet (tape–recorded)

Can you tell me about any face-to-face contact you have had with the client during this week?

> [Probes: How much time did you spend with the client?
> Where were you?
> Who else was there?
> What happened?
> Why did you do what you did?
> Who made the decisions?
> What were you trying to achieve?
> What are you going to do next?]

Can you tell me about any discussions you have had with anyone this week about the client?

> [Probes: How much time did you spend on this?
> Where did it take place?
> Was it by telephone?
> Who was involved?
> What happened?
> Why did you have this discussion(s)?
> Who made the decisions?
> What were you (or others) trying to achieve?
> What did you do/are you going to do as a result of the discussion(s)?]

Can you tell me about any other direct or indirect involvement you have had with this client during this week?

> [Probes: How much time did you spend on this?
> Where did it take place?
> Who was involved?
> What happened?
> Why did this happen?
> Who made the decisions?
> What were you (or others) trying to achieve?
> What did you do/are you going to do as a result of this?]

If you have had no direct or indirect involvement with the client during this week, could you tell me why?

> [Probes: Why did this happen?
> Who made the decision not to have any involvement?
> What were you trying to achieve?]

CPN–referral 'action' data (data extracted from tape-recordings)

1. CPN no.   [ ] [ ]
2. Team no.   [ ]
53. Referral no.   [ ] [ ]
54. Week no. (1–15)   [ ] [ ]
73. Time spent on any direct contact:
      (1) None   [ ] [ ]
      (2) Less than one hour   [ ]
      (3) One hour or more but less than two   [ ]
      (4) Two hours or more   [ ]

74. Location of any direct contact:
      (1) Client's home   [ ]
      (2) CPN centre   [ ]
      (3) Day centre   [ ]
      (4) Ward   [ ]
      (5) Relative's home   [ ] [ ]
      (6) Hostel   [ ]
      (7) Out-patients clinic   [ ]
      (8) Other   [ ]
Notes:

75. Participants in any direct contact:
      (1) CPN and client only   [ ]
      (2) CPN, colleague and client   [ ]
      (3) CPN, student and client   [ ] [ ]
      (4) CPN, client and member of family/friend   [ ]
      (5) Other   [ ]
Notes:

76. Therapeutic style used in any direct contact:
      (1) Assessment   [ ]
      (2) Counselling   [ ]
      (3) Giving medication   [ ]
      (4) Other physical care   [ ]
      (5) Advising   [ ]
      (6) Education   [ ] [ ] [ ]
      (7) Specialist therapy   [ ]
      (8) Reassurance/support   [ ]
      (9) Monitoring   [ ]
      (10) Evaluating   [ ]

(11) Unspecified   [ ]
(12) Other   [ ]

Notes:

Discussions held with:
77. No-one   [ ]
78. Consultant psychiatrist   [ ]
79. Other member of the psychiatric medical team   [ ]
80. GP   [ ]
81. Medical practitioner other than above   [ ]
82. Social worker   [ ]
83. Psychologist   [ ]
84. Occupational therapist   [ ]
85. CPN   [ ]
86. District nurse   [ ]
87. Health visitor   [ ]
88. Team leader   [ ]
89. Supervisor   [ ]
90. Manager   [ ]
91. Voluntary agency   [ ]
92. Other (e.g. student/relatives)   [ ]

Notes:

93. Other involvement (asked as an open question):
    (1) None   [ ]
    (2) Client not in/not turn up   [ ]
    (3) Telephone conversation with client/letter   [ ]
    (4) CPN on holiday   [ ]
    (5) Discharged/transferred etc.   [ ]
    (6) Letter to consultant/GP   [ ] [ ] [ ]
    (7) Visit by student/colleague   [ ]
    (8) Discussed with CMHT   [ ]
    (9) CPN sick   [ ]
    (10) CPN sick but client visited by
        student/colleague   [ ]

Appendix 2

Focused–interview Schedule

Interviewee:

Date:

Area:

Notes:

Aims
1. To assess the professional 'status' of the CPN as viewed by her/his mental health colleagues.
2. To evaluate the role of the CPN as perceived by her/his mental health colleagues.
3. To establish the degree of collegiality, conflict and rivalry that exists between the CPN and her/his mental health colleagues.
4. To monitor any 'ideological' incompatibility between the CPN and her/his mental health colleagues, and identify the existence of possible 'hegemonisation'.
5. To evaluate the level of supervisory/managerial control and/or the existence of overt/covert hierarchies affecting the role of the CPN.

Key probe headings	Probe categories
What	CPN role
Where	Role comparisons
How	Referrals – CPN autonomy
When	Hierarchical/supervisory
Why	Structures
Who	Organisational structure
	Ideal types

1. CPN role (general and comparative)

a. What do you consider the role of the CPN to be?
b. How does that role differ from your own? (attitudes; skills; knowledge; status; levels of autonomy; legal elements; codes of conduct etc.).
c. In what way does the role of the CPN differ from that of other mental health workers (e.g. social worker; psychiatrist; psychologist; occupational therapist)?

2. CPNs and the referral process

a. Who should CPNs accept referrals from? (Why?)
b. How much control should CPNs have over who they accept as a referral?
c. What are your views about the role of the CPN in assessing clients?
d. What are your views about CPNs independently carrying out the initial assessment of clients?
e. What are your views about CPNs independently organising treatment or care programmes for clients?
f. What are your views about CPNs independently implementing treatment or care programmes for clients?
g. How much control should CPNs have over discharging clients from their case-load?

3. Hierarchical/supervisory structures

a. What are your views on the 'supervision of CPNs'?
b. What do you mean by 'supervision'?
c. Who do you feel should supervise CPNs?
d. How should CPNs be supervised?
e. Why should CPNs be supervised?
f. Who should CPNs be responsible to, and for what? clinically; managerially.

4. Organisational structures

a. Where do you feel it is best to have CPNs located (e.g. PHCTs; CMHTs; hospital based)?
b. What are your reasons for this?

5. Ideal types

a. What makes a 'good' CPN?
b. What makes a 'bad' CPN?

c. What needs to happen to improve CPN practice?

Is there anything you would like to add?

Appendix 3

Field notebook

Team:

Research week:

Date:

Time:

Substantive observations

Methodological observations

Analytical comments

References
and Bibliography

Abbott P, Wallace C (Eds) (1990) The Sociology of the Caring Professions. London: Falmer Press. **pp.9, 33, 39**

Abel-Smith B (1960) A History of the Nursing Profession. London: Heinemann. **p.34**

Abercrombie N, Hill S, Turner BS (1994) (3rd edn) The Penguin Dictionary of Sociology. Harmondsworth: Penguin. **p.3**

Abraham J (1995) Science, Politics and the Pharmaceutical Industry. London: University College London Press. **p.28**

Adams GR, Schvaneveldt (1985) Understanding Research Methods. New York: Longman. **pp.63, 64**

Adler PA, Adler P (1987) Membership Roles in Field Research. Beverly Hills, USA: Sage. **p.60**

Althusser L (1969) For Marx. London: Allen Lane. **p.41**

Anleu SLR (1992) The professionalisation of social work? A case study of three organisational settings. Sociology 26 (1): 23–43.

Antaki C (Ed) (1988) Analysing Everyday Explanation: A Casebook of Methods. London: Sage.

Archer J (1985) Brindle House – case history. Community Psychiatric Nursing Journal 5 (6): 16–17.

Argyle M (1983) (4th edn) The Psychology of Interpersonal Behaviour. Harmondsworth: Penguin.

Armstrong D (1983) The Political Anatomy of the Body. Cambridge: Cambridge University Press.

Armstrong D (1990) Medicine as a profession: times of change. British Medical Journal 301: 3 October, 691–3. **pp.7, 16, 18**

Armstrong J (1987) Community Health Nurses – the frontline workers. Canadian Journal of Psychiatric Nursing 28 (4): 4–6. **p.48**

Ashdown AM (1943) (2nd edn) A Complete System of Nursing. London: Dent.**p.34**

Ashmore M, Mulkay M, Pinch T (1989) Health and Efficiency: A Sociology of Health Economics. Buckingham: Open University Press. **p.31**

Atkinson HW (1988) Head in the clouds, feet on the ground. Physiotherapy 74 (11): 542–7. **p.33**

Atkinson P (1990) The Ethnographic Imagination: Textual Constructions of Reality. London: Routledge.

Audit Commission (1994) Finding a Place: A Review of Mental Health Services for Adults. London: HMSO. **pp.114, 115, 116, 125, 126**

Baggott R (1994) Health and Health Care in Britain. Basingstoke: Macmillan **pp.24, 41**

Bailey KD (1978) Methods of Social Research. New York: Free Press.

Barber B (1963) Some problems in the sociology of the professions. Daedalus 92: 669–88. **p.8**

Barbie E (1989) (5th edn) The Practice of Social Research. Belmont, California: Wadsworth.

Barker P (1995) Promoting growth through community mental health nursing. Mental Health Nursing 15 (3): 12–15.

Barker P, Baldwin S, Ulas M (1989) Medical expansionism: some implications for psychiatric nursing practice. Nurse Education Today 9: 192–202.

Barker P, Jackson S (1997) Mental health nursing: making it a primary concern. Nursing Standard 11 (17): 39–41. **pp.117, 118, 124**

Barnes R (1990) Challenging public fears of madness. Nursing Standard 4 (49): 7–8. **p.113**

Barratt E (1989) Community psychiatric nurses: their self-perceived roles. Journal of Advanced Nursing 14: 42–8. **pp.48, 64, 82**

Baruch G, Treacher A (1978) Psychiatry Observed. London: Routledge and Kegan Paul. **pp.17, 45**

Bean P (1979) Psychiatrists' assessments of mental illness: a comparison of Thomas Scheff's approach to labelling theory. British Journal of Psychiatry 135: 122–8.

Bean P (1980) Compulsory Admissions to Mental Hospitals. Chichester: Wiley.

Bean P (1983) (Ed) Mental Illness: Changes and Trends. Chichester: Wiley.

Bean P (1993) Tipping care towards social control. The Guardian, 24 February. **pp.56, 87, 119**

Bean P, Mounser P (1993) Discharged from Mental Hospitals. London: Macmillan/MIND. **pp.18, 50, 52**

Beard PG (1980) Community psychiatric nursing: a challenging role. Nursing Focus 1: 15–18. **pp.48, 54**

Beard PG (1984) The nursing element in an ideal service. In Reed J, Lomas G (Eds) Psychiatric Services in the Community. London: Croom Helm.

Becker HS (1958) Problems or inference and proof in participant observation. American Sociological Review 23(6): 652–60, quoted in Burgess R G (Ed) (1982) Field Research: a Sourcebook and Field Manual. London: George Allen and Unwin.

Bell D (1973) The Coming of Post-Industrial Society. New York: Basic Books.7

Bell J (1987) Doing Your Research Project. Milton Keynes: Open University Press.

Benney M, Hughes EC (1984) Of Sociology and the interview. In Bulmer M (Ed) (2nd edn) Sociological Research Methods: An Introduction. London: Macmillan.

Benoit C (1989) The professional socialisation of midwives: balancing art and science. Sociology of Health and Illness 11 (2): 160–80. **p.39**

Berens C (1995) What's up Doc? The Guardian, 15 August. **p.30**

Berger P, Luckmann T (1967) The Social Construction of Reality. London: Allen Lane.

Berlant JL (1975) Professions and Monopoly: a Study of Medicine in the United States and Great Britain. Berkeley: University of California Press. **p.17**

Bevins A (1993) Doctors' blunders may face glare of public scrutiny. The Observer, 22 August. **p.20**

Bhaskar R (1979) The Possibility of Naturalism: A Philosophical Critique of the Contemporary Human Sciences. Brighton: Harvester.

Black E, John WG (1986) Leadership of the multi-disciplinary team in psychiatry – a nursing perspective. Nursing Practice 1: 177–82. **p.55**

Blane D (1993) Clinical Sociology: What Might it Be? In Payne G, Cross M (Eds)

Sociology in Action. Basingstoke: Macmillan/British Sociological Association. pp. 57–68. **p.126**

Blom-Cooper L, Hally H, Murphy E (1995) The Falling Shadow: One Patient's Mental Health Care 1978–1993. London: Duckworth. **p.126**

Blom-Cooper L, Grounds A, Guinan P, Parker A, Taylor M (1996) The Case of Jason Mitchell: Report of the Independent Panel of Inquiry. London: Duckworth. **pp.81, 115**

Borger J (1994) Madness hidden in impassive hills. The Guardian, 31 December. **pp.124, 125**

Bowers L (1992) A preliminary description of the United Kingdom community psychiatric nursing literature, 1960–1990. Journal of Advanced Nursing 17: 739–46.

Boyd W (1994) Chairman of Steering Committee of the Confidential Enquiry into Homicides and Suicides by Mentally Ill People – A Preliminary Report on Homicide. London: Royal College of Psychiatrists. **p.119**

Boyd W (1996) (Director) Report of the Confidential Inquiry into Homicides and Suicides by Mentally Ill People. London: Royal College of Psychiatrists. **p.121**

Boyle M (1993) Schizophrenia – A Scientific Delusion. London: Routledge. **p.28**

Brackx A, Grimshaw C (Eds) (1989) Mental Health Care in Crisis. London: Pluto.

Brewer J, Hunter A (1989) Multimethod Research: A Synthesis of Styles. London: Sage.

Briggs CL (1986) Learning How to Ask: A Sociolinguistic Appraisal of the Role of the Interview in Social Science Research. Cambridge: Cambridge University Press. **p.62**

Brindle D (1993a) Into the cold or the community. The Guardian, 24 February.**p.56**

Brindle D (1993b) Bottomley's mental health plans flawed. The Guardian, 8 July. **p.56**

Brindle D (1993c) Mentally ill will be registered on discharge. The Guardian, 28 December.

Brindle D (1994a) Named nurse scheme fails publicity test. The Guardian, 25 April. **pp.30, 36**

Brindle D (1994b) GPs rid lists of difficult patients. The Guardian, 11 July. **pp.30, 125**

Brindle D (1994c) Schizophrenic's death fuels community care fear. The Guardian, 2 June. **p.113**

Brindle D (1994d) Psychiatrists slated on killing by patient. The Guardian, 4 November. **p.119**

Brindle D (1995a) A tricky question of trust. The Guardian, 15 January. **p.25**

Brindle D (1995b) Doctors win local rates fight. The Guardian, 7 February. **p.25**

Brindle D (1996) Torments of the mentally ill: survey finds 'staggering' level of bias, harassment and abuse. The Guardian, 25 November. **p.125**

Brindle D (1997) Doctors ahead of NHS fat cats. The Guardian, 17 February. **p.32**

Brindle D, Mihill C (1994) Doctors threaten to opt out of NHS to avoid DIKTAT. The Guardian, 23 March. **p.25**

Brooker C (Ed) (1990) Community Psychiatric Nursing: A Research Perspective. London: Chapman & Hall.

Brooker C (1990) A six-year follow-up study of nurses attending a course in community psychiatric nursing. In Brooker C (Ed) (1990) Community Psychiatric Nursing: A Research Perspective. London: Chapman & Hall. **pp. 252–78.**

Brooker C, Butterworth T (1991) Working with families caring for a relative with schizophrenia: the evolving role of the community psychiatric nurse.

International Journal of Nursing Studies 28 (2): 189–200. **p.117**

Brooker C, Butterworth T (1993) Training in psychosocial intervention: the impact on the role of community psychiatric nurses. Journal of Advanced Nursing 18 (4): 583–90. **p.118**

Brooker CGD, Simmons S (1985) A study to compare two models of community psychiatric nursing care delivery. Journal of Advanced Nursing 10: 217–23. **p.52**

Brooker C, White EG (Eds) (1993) Community Psychiatric Nursing: A Research Perspective Volume 2. London: Chapman & Hall.

Brooker C, White E (1995) Community Psychiatric Nursing: A Research Perspective, Volume 3. London: Chapman & Hall. **p.49**

Brooker C, Repper J, Booth A (1996) Examining effectiveness of community mental health nursing. Mental Health Nursing 16 (3): 12–15.

Bryman A (1988) Quality and Quantity in Social Research. London: Unwin Hyman. **p.61**

Bryman A, Cramer D (1990) Quantitative Data Analysis for Social Scientists. London: Routledge.

Bucher R (1962) Pathology: a study of social movements within a profession. Social Problems 19: 40–51. **p.39**

Bucher R, Stelling J (1969) Characteristics of professional organisation. Journal of Health and Social Behaviour 10 (1): 3–15. **p.19**

Bucher R, Strauss A (1961) Professions in process. American Journal of Sociology 66 (4): 325–34. **pp.19, 39**

Burgess RG (1981) Keeping a research diary. Cambridge Journal of Education 11, part 1: 75–83. **p.67**

Burgess RG (Ed) (1982) Field Research: a Source and Field Manual. London: Allen and Unwin.

Burgess RG (1983) Experiencing Comprehensive Education : A Study of Bishop McGregor School. London: Methuen. **p.63**

Burgess RG (1984) In the Field: An Introduction to Field Research. London: Unwin Hyman.

Burgess RG (1990) British Sociological Association Presidential Address 1990: sociologists, training and research. Sociology 24 (4): 579–95.

Burnard P (1991) A method of analysing interview scripts in qualitative research. Nurse Education Today 11: 461–6. **p.74**

Burrows R, Loader B (1994) Towards a Post Fordist Welfare State? London: Routledge. **p.24**

Bury M (1995) The body in question: 1995 Medical Sociology Plenary. Medical Sociology News 21 (1): 36–48. **p.29**

Busfield J (1986) Managing Madness: Changing Ideas and Practice. London: Unwin Hyman. **p.12**

Butterworth T (1984) The future training of psychiatric and general nurses. Nursing Times, 80(30) 65–6. **p.39**

Butterworth T, Faugier J (Eds) (1992) Clinical Supervision and Mentorship in Nursing. London: Chapman & Hall. **p.100**

Buttifant B (1986) The Alexandra Resource Centre, Great Yarmouth. Community Psychiatric Nursing Journal 6 (2): 13–15.

Campbell DT (1969) Perspective: artifact and control. In Rosenthal R, Rosnow R L (Eds) Artifact in Behavioral Research. New York: Academic Press.

Campbell DT, Fiske DW (1959) Convergent and discriminate validation by the multitrait-multimethod matrix. Psychological Bulletin 54: 297–312.

Campbell DT, Stanley TD (1963) Experimental and Quasi-experimental Designs for Research. Chicago: Rand McNally.

Campbell W, Dixon A, Dow I (1983) A case for a new training. Nursing Mirror 156: 42–6.

Carchedi G (1975) On the economic identification of the new middle class. Economy and Society 4 (1): 1–85. **p.12**

Carkhuff RR, Anthony WA (1979) The Skills of Helping: An Introduction to Counselling. Amherst, Mass.: Human Resource Development Press.

Carr PJ, Butterworth CA, Hodges BE (1980) Community Psychiatric Nursing. London: Churchill Livingstone. **pp.23, 48, 54**

Carr-Saunders AM, Wilson PA (1933) The Professions. Oxford: Clarendon Press. **p.8**

Cartwright FF (1977) A Social History of Medicine. London: Longman. **p.43**

Cicourel AV (1964) Method and Measurement in Sociology. New York: Free Press.

Cicourel AV (1974) Cognitive Sociology: Language and Meaning in Social Interaction. New York: Free Press.

Cicourel AV (1982) Interviews and surveys, and the problem of ecological validity. American Sociologist 17: 11–20.

Clare A (1976) Psychiatry in Dissent. London: Tavistock. **pp.28, 51**

Clarke J, Layder D (1994) Let's get real: the realist approach in sociology. Sociology Review November: 6–9.

Clegg F (1982) Simple Statistics. Cambridge: Cambridge University Press.

Clegg S (1989) Frameworks of Power. London: Sage. **p.24**

Coghlan A (1994) Software tycoons back drugs from genes. New Scientist 142 (1925): 4. **p.27**

Cohen D (1988) Forgotten Millions: The Treatment of the Mentally Ill – a Global Perspective. London: Paladin. **pp.53, 124**

Cohen S (1972/80) Folk Devils and Moral Panics: The Creation of the Mods and the Rockers. Oxford: Basil Blackwell.

Collee J (1995) Medicine. The Observer Magazine, 31 December. **p.20**

Commons Health Committee (1992/93) Community Supervision Orders – Fifth Report. London: HMSO.

Community Psychiatric Nurses Association (1985) The 1985 CPNA National Survey Update. CPNA: Bristol. **p.48**

Cook TD, Campbell DT (1979) Quasi-Experimentation: Design and Analysis Issues for the Field Settings. Chicago: Rand McNally. **p.71**

Cooper G (1995) How many more deaths, asks daughter. The Independent 26 September. **p.121**

Cooper G (1996a) Care in the community. The Independent, 7 March.

Cooper G (1996b) Nurses replace doctors in 24-hour calls trial. The Independent, 3 January. **p.38**

Corbin M (1971) Problems and procedures of interviewing. In Phal JM, Phal RE (Eds) Managers and Their Wives. London: Allen Lane.

Coward R (1992) Are you really going mental? The Observer, 22 November. **p.113**

Craig T, Bayliss E, Klein O, Manning P, Reader L (1995) The Homeless Mentally Ill Initiative: An Evaluation of Four Clinical Teams. London: Department of Health/Mental Health Foundation. **p.11**

Crichton J (1995) Psychiatric Patient Violence: Risk and Response. London: Duckworth.

Crook S, Pakulski J, Waters M (1992) Postmodernization: Change in Advanced Society. London: Sage.

Cross D, Morrall PA (1991) Starting a community psychiatric nursing course in a log cabin. Community Psychiatric Nursing Journal 11 (4): 22–7.

Cumberlege Report (1986) Neighbourhood Nursing – A Focus for Care. Report of the Community Nursing Review. London: HMSO. **p.53**

Davidson B (1992) What can be the relevance of the psychiatric nurse to the life of a person who is mentally ill? Journal of Clinical Nursing 1: 199–205.

Davidson L (Ed) (1990) News – call for practice review. Nursing Times 86 (39): 8.

Davies C (1996) The sociology of the professions and the profession of gender. Sociology 30 (4): 661–78. **p.34**

Dean EA (1988) Evaluation of the Community Psychiatric Nursing Service: Tunbridge Wells Health Authority. Unpublished report. **pp.53, 54, 55**

Denzin N (1970) The Research Act. Chicago: Aldine. **p.71**

Department of Health (1989a) Working for Patients. London: HMSO. **pp.26, 56**

Department of Health (1989b) Caring for People: Community Care in the Next Decade and Beyond. London: HMSO. **p.56**

Department of Health (1990a) The National Health Service and Community Care Act. London: HMSO.

Department of Health (1990b) The Care Programme Approach for people with a mental illness referred to the specialist psychiatric services. HC(90)23/LASSL(90)11. London: Department of Health. **p.56**

Department of Health (1991) The Health of a Nation. London: HMSO.

Department of Health (1994a) National Health Service Workforce in England. London: HMSO.

Department of Health (1994b) Working in Partnership: A Collaborative Approach to Care. Report of the Mental Health Nursing Review Team (Chairperson: Butterworth T). London: HMSO. **pp.56, 100, 116, 117, 126**

Department of Health (1997) Green Consultation Paper: Developing Partnerships in Mental Health. London: HMSO. **p.56**

Department of Health and Home Office (1992) Review of Health and Social Services for Mentally Disordered Offenders and Others Requiring Similar Services (The Reed Report). London: HMSO. **p.121**

Department of Health and Social Security (1984) 5th Report of The Steering Group on Health Services Information (Chairperson: Korner E). London: HMSO.

Department of Health and Welsh Office (1983) The Mental Health Act 1983. London: HMSO. **p.56**

Department of Health and Welsh Office (1993) The Mental Health Act 1983 Code of Practice (revised). London: HMSO. **p.56**

Derber C (Ed) (1982) Professionals as Workers: Mental Labour in Advanced Capitalism. Boston: Hall. **p.12**

Derber C (1984) Managing professionals: ideological proletarianization and post-industrial labor. Theory and Society 12: 309–41.

Deutscher I (1984) Asking Questions (and listening to answers): a review of some sociological precedents and problems. In Bulmer M (Ed) (2nd edn) Sociological Research Methods: An Introduction. London: Macmillan.

Devlin R (1985) Training for the front line. Nursing Times 81 (20): 19–20.

Dexter G, Morrall PA (1987) All dressed up and nowhere to go: implications for the future of CPN education. Community Psychiatric Nursing Journal 7 (4): 11–15.

Dexter G, Wash M (1986) Psychiatric Nursing Skills: A Patient-Centred Approach. London: Croom Helm. **pp.47, 121**

Dingwall R (1974) Some sociological aspects of nursing research. Sociological Review 22 (1): 45–55. **pp.38, 55**

Dingwall R (1986) Anatomy of a profession: training for a varied career. Nursing Times 82(13) 27–8. **p.33**

Dingwall R, Lewis P (Eds) (1983) The Sociology of the Professions: Lawyers,

Doctors and Others. London: Macmillan. **pp.7, 34**

Dingwall R, Strong PM (1985) The interactionist study of organisations: A critique and reformulation. Urban Life 14 (2): 205–31.

Dingwall R, Rafferty AM, Webster C (1988) An Introduction to the Social History of Nursing. London: Routledge. **pp.39, 47**

Dixon M (1992) Locating the manger inside the doctor. The Guardian 23 September. **p.24**

Dunleavy P (1987) Studying for a Degree. London: Macmillan.

Durkheim E (1957) Professional Ethics and Civil Morals. London: Routledge and Kegan Paul. **p.7**

Duxbury J (1996) The nurse's role as patient advocate for mentally ill people. Nursing Standard 10 (20): 36–9. **p.121**

Eastman N (1994) Mental health law: civil liberties and the principal of reciprocity. British Medical Journal 308 (January): 43–5. **p.87**

Egan G (1986) (3rd edn) The Skilled Helper: A Systematic Approach to Effective Helping. Belmont, California: Brooks/Cole.

Egan G (1991) (4th edn) The Skilled Helper: A Systematic Approach to Effective Helping. Belmont, California: Brooks/Cole.

Ehrenreich B, English D (1976) Complaints and Disorders: The Sexual Politics of Sickness. London: Writers and Readers Publishing Cooperative.

Elston MA (1991) The politics of professional power: medicine in a changing health care service. In Gabe J, Calnan M, Bury M (Eds) The Sociology of the Health Service. London: Routledge. pp. 58–88. **pp.20, 30**

English National Board for Nursing, Midwifery and Health Visiting (1985) Nursing Care of Mentally Ill People in the Community: Course Number 811 (Outline Curriculum). London: ENB.

English National Board for Nursing, Midwifery and Health Visiting (1989a) Nursing Care of Mentally Ill People in the Community: Course Number 812 (Outline Curriculum). London: ENB. **p.50**

English National Board for Nursing, Midwifery and Health Visiting (1989b) Project 2000 – A New Preparation for Practice. London: ENB.

English National Board for Nursing, Midwifery and Health Visiting (1995) Press release: approval of two new education programmes relating to expanding roles for nurses (N77 Nurse as assistant to the surgeon, and N78 Intra-articular and soft tissue injection techniques for nurses). London: ENB. **p.38**

English National Board for Nursing, Midwifery and Health Visiting (1996) Regulations for the Approval of Institutions and Programmes. London: ENB. **p.126**

English and Welsh Boards for Nursing, Midwifery, and Health Visiting (1982) Syllabus of Training, Professional Register – Part 3 (Registered Mental Nurse). London/Cardiff: ENB/WNB. **p.76**

Etzioni A (Ed) (1969) The Semi-Professions and their Organisation. New York: Free Press. **p.33**

Fahy P (1994) Autonomy and decision making in community psychiatric nurses. The International Journal of Psychiatric Nursing Research 1 (2): 41–8. **p.57**

Field PA, Morse JM (1985) Nursing Research: The Application of Qualitative Approaches. London: Chapman & Hall.

Fielding NG, Fielding JL (1986) Linking Data. Beverly Hills, California: Sage.

Filstead WJ (1970) Qualitative Methodology: Firsthand Involvement with the Social World. Chicago: Markham.

Filstead WJ (1979) Qualitative methods: a needed perspective in evaluation research. In Cook TD, Reichardt CS (Eds) Qualitative and Quantitative Methods in Evaluation Research. Beverly Hills, California: Sage.

Finch J (1984) 'It's great to have someone to talk to': the ethics and politics of interviewing women. In Bell C, Roberts H (Eds) Social Researching: Policies, Problems, Practice. London: Routledge and Kegan Paul.

Fletcher D (1995) Care of mentally ill 'in state of turmoil'. The Electronic Telegraph, 25 August. **p.2**

Fletcher D (1996) Call to replace nurses with 'health workers'. The Daily Telegraph, 23 May. **pp.41, 42**

Foucault M (1967) Madness and Civilisation – a History of Insanity in the Age of Reason. London: Tavistock. **pp.12, 44, 50**

Foucault M (1970) The Order of Things: An Archaeology of the Human Sciences. New York: Pantheon.

Foucault M (1972) The Archaeology of Knowledge. New York: Pantheon.

Foucault M (1973) The Birth of the Clinic: An Archaeology of Medical Perception. New York: Pantheon. **p.12**

Foucault M (1980) Power/Knowledge: Selected Interviews and Other Writings 1972–1977. New York: Pantheon.

Fowler R (1996) Aromatherapists pour oils on troubled ailments. The Independent, 12 August. **p.21**

Fox NJ (1992) The Social Meaning of Surgery. Buckingham: Open University Press. **p.13**

Fox NJ (1993) Postmodernism, Sociology and Health. Buckingham: Open University Press. **p.13**

Freddi G, Bjorkman JW (Eds) (1989) Controlling Medical Professionals: The Comparative Politics of Health Governance. London: Sage.

Freedland J (1994) A network in your own front room. The Guardian Outlook, 30 April. **p.26**

Freidson E (Ed) (1963) The Hospital in Modern Society. London: Macmillan.

Freidson E (1970a) The Profession of Medicine: A Study of the Sociology of Applied Knowledge. New York: Dodd, Mead. **pp.13, 17, 31, 33, 38, 43**

Freidson E (1970b) Professional Dominance: The Social Structure of Medical Care. Chicago: Aldine. **pp.13, 15, 17, 31, 33, 43, 58, 103, 111**

Freidson E (1976) The division of labour as social interaction. Social Problems 23 (February): 304–13.

Freidson E (1978) The official construction of work: an essay on the practical epistemology of occupations. Paper presented at the Ninth World Congress of Sociology, Upsala.

Freidson E (1986) Professional Powers: A Study of the Institutionalisation of Formal Knowledge. Chicago: University of Chicago Press. **p.19**

Freidson E (1988) The Profession of Medicine: A study of the Sociology of Applied Knowledge – With a New Afterword. Chicago: University of Chicago Press. **pp.13, 17, 25, 26, 30–31, 52, 58, 66**

Freidson E (1994) Professionalism Reborn: Theory, Prophecy and Policy. Cambridge: Polity Press. **p.25**

Gabe J, Kelleher D, Williams G (1994) Challenging Medicine. London: Routledge. **p.31**

Gamarnikow E (1978) Sexual division of labour: the case of nursing. In Kuhn A, Wolpe A (Eds) Feminism and Materialism: Women and Modes of Production. London: Routledge and Kegan Paul. pp. 96–123. **pp.8, 35**

Game A, Pringle R (1983) Gender at Work. Sydney: Allen & Unwin. **p.35**

General Nursing Council for England and Wales (1982) Training Syllabus Register of Mental Training. London: GNC.

Gibson CH (1991) A concept analysis of empowerment. Journal of Advanced Nursing 16: 354–61. **p.126**

Giddens A (1990) The Consequences of Modernity. Cambridge: Polity Press. **p.7**

Giddens A (1991) Modernity and Self-identity: Self and Society in the Late Modern Age. Cambridge: Polity Press. **p.7**

Glaser B, Strauss A (1967) (tenth printing) The Discovery of Grounded Theory: Strategies for Qualitative Research. New York: Aldine.

Godin P (1996) The development of community psychiatric nursing: a professional project?' Journal of Advanced Nursing 23 (5): 925–34. **p.48**

Goffman E (1959) The Presentation of Self in Everyday Life. Harmondsworth: Penguin. **p.69**

Goffman E (1962) Asylums: Essays on the Social Situation of Mental Patients and Other Inmates. New York: Doubleday.

Goldberg D, Huxley P (1992) Common Mental Disorders: A Biosocial Model. London: Tavistock/Routledge.

Goldie N (1974) Professional Processes Among Three Occupational Groups within the Mental Health Field. Unpublished PhD thesis. London: City University.

Goldie N (1977) The division of labour among mental health professions – a negotiated or an imposed order?. In Stacey M et al (Eds) Health and the Division of Labour. London: Croom Helm. pp. 141–61. **p.19**

Goode E (Ed) (1996) Social Deviance. Needham Heights, USA: Allyn and Bacon.

Goode WJ (1957) Community within a community: the professions. American Sociological Review 22: 194–200. **p.8**

Goode WJ (1960) Encroachment, charlatanism, and the emerging profession: psychiatry, sociology, and medicine. American Sociological Review 25: 902–14.

Gough I (1979) Political Economy of the Welfare State. London: Macmillan. **p.12**

Gournay K (1990) A return to the medical model? Nursing Times 86 (40): 46–7. **p.118**

Gournay K (1994) Redirecting the emphasis to serious mental illness. Nursing Times 90 (25): 40–1. **pp.56, 118**

Greene J (1968) The psychiatric nurse in the community. International Journal of Nursing Studies 5, 175–83. **p.48**

Greenwood E (1957) Attributes of a profession. Social Work 2: 44–55. **p.8**

Greer S, Greer AL (1984) The continuity of moral reform: community mental health centres. Social Science and Medicine 19 (4): 397–404. **p.53**

Grice E (1996) Living in fear of a schizophrenic son. The Daily Telegraph, 24 April. **p.123**

Griffiths P, Evans A (1995) Evaluating a Nursing-led Service: an Interim Report. Poole: Bournemouth English Book Centre/King's Fund. **p.37**

Griffiths R (1988) (Chairperson) Community Care: Agenda for Action. London: HMSO. **p.56**

Gross E (1958) Work and Society. New York: Thomas Crowell. **p.8**

Guardian (1993) Mental health law review ordered after lion attack. 4 January.

Habermas J (1970) Towards a Rational Society. London: Heinemann.

Habermas J (1972) Knowledge and Human Interests. London: Heinemann.

Hally H (1989) All in a day's work. Community Outlook, 6–11 January, 4–6. **p.49**

Hally H (1994) Myths, legends and the future in the community. Primary Health Care 4 (7): 6–11. **pp.113, 119**

Hammersley M (1990) What's wrong with ethnography? The myth of theoretical description. Sociology 24 (4): 597–615.

Hammersley M (1992) What's Wrong With Ethnography? London: Routledge.

Hammersley M, Atkinson P (1995) (2nd edn) Ethnography: Principles in Practice. London: Routledge. **p.60**

Harrison S, Hunter D, Pollitt C (1990) The Dynamics of British Health Policy. London: Unwin Hyman. **p.21**

Harrison S, Pollitt C (1994) Controlling Health Professionals: the Future of Work and Organisation in the NHS. Buckingham: Open University Press. **p.24**

Hart E (1991) Ghost in the machine. Health Services Journal. 5 December: 20–2. **p.38**

Haug M (1973) De-professionalisation: an alternative hypothesis for the future. In Halmos P (Ed) Professionalisation and Social Change. Sociological Review Monograph 20: Keele: University of Keele. 195–212. **p.12**

Haug M (1975) The deprofessionalization of everyone? Sociological Focus, August: 197–213.

Haug MB (1988) A re-examination of the hypothesis of deprofessionalisation. Milbank Quarterly, supplement 2: 48–56. **p.20**

Hawkins P, Shohet R (1989) Supervision in the Helping Professions. Buckingham: Open University Press. **p.100**

Haywood S (1987) Not what the ministers ordered. The Times, 22 April. **p.24**

Health Committee (House of Commons) (1994) Better Off in the Community? The Care of People who are Seriously Mentally Ill. Volume 1. London: HMSO. **pp.113, 114, 126**

Hearn HL (1968) Identity and institutional imperatives: the socialisation of student actresses. Sociological Quarterly 9: 47–63.

Hearn J (1982) Notes on patriarchy, professionalisation and the semi-professions. Sociology 16 (2): 184–202. **p.8**

Henderson V (1966) The Nature of Nursing. New York: Macmillan. **p.35**

Hollingwood J, Rickard I (1994) Counselling and the role of the mental health nurse. Mental Health Nursing 14 (1): 9–13.

Horrocks P (1985) Memorandum to Social Services Committee on Community Care with Special Reference to Adult Mentally Ill and Mentally Handicapped People, on behalf of the NHS Health Advisory Service. London: HMSO. **p.111**

Hughes D (1988) When nurse knows best: some aspects of nurse/doctor interaction in a casualty department. Sociology of Health and Illness 10 (1): 1–22. **pp.23, 52, 105**

Hughes EC (1958) Men and their Work. Glencoe, Illinois: Free Press. **p.13**

Hughes EC (1971) The Sociological Eye. Chicago: Aldine. **pp.37, 103**

Hughes G (1991) Taking crime seriously? A critical analysis of New Left Realism. Sociology Review, November: 18–23.

Hugman R (1991) Power in Caring Professions. London: Macmillan. **p.21**

Hunt G, Wainwright P (Eds) (1994) Expanding the Role of the Nurse: The Scope of Professional Practice. Oxford: Blackwell. **pp.34, 36, 37, 40**

Hunt M, Mangan J (1990) Information for practice through computerised records. In Brooker C (Ed) Community Psychiatric Nursing: a Research Perspective. London: Chapman & Hall. pp. 95–112. **p.99**

Hunter D (1991) Managing medicine: a response to crisis. Social Science and Medicine 32: 441–8. **p.24**

Hunter P (1974) Community psychiatric nursing in Britain: an historical review. International Journal of Nursing Studies 2(4), 223–33. **p.48**

Illich I (1977) Limits To Medicine. Harmondsworth: Penguin. **p.10**

Illich I, Zola IK, McKnight J, Caplan J, Shaiken H (1977) Disabling Professions. Boston: Marion Boyers. **p.10**

Illing J, Drinkwater C, Roger T, Forster D, Rutherford P (1990) Evaluation of Community Psychiatric Nursing in General Practice. In Brooker C. (Ed) Community Psychiatric Nursing: a Research Perspective. London: Chapman & Hall, pp. 144–73. **p.111**

Illman J (1991) Not enough patient power in the waiting rooms. The Guardian, 29 March. **p.30**

Illman J (1993) Catching up with the charlatans of the couch. The Guardian, 25 May. **p.118**

Illman J (1996) Power of spiritual healing. The Guardian, 29 October. **p.21**

Jamous J, Peloille B (1970) Professions or self perpetuating systems? Changes in the French University Hospital system. In Jackson J (Ed) Professions and Professionalism. Cambridge: Cambridge University Press. pp. 111–52. **p.16**

Johnson S, Ramsay R, Thornicroft G, Brooks L, Lelliott P, Peck E, Smith H, Chisholm D, Audini B, Knapp M, Goldberg D (Eds) (1997) London's Mental Health: The Report to the King's Fund London Commission. London: King's Fund. **pp.114, 125, 126**

Johnson T (1972) Professions and Power. London: Macmillan. **p.7,8,13**

Johnson T (1977) The professions in the class structure. In Scase D (Ed) Industrial Society: Class, Cleavage and Control. London: Allen and Unwin. pp. 93–110. **p.12**

Johnstone L (1989) Users and Abusers of Psychiatry: A Critical Look at Traditional Psychiatric Practice. London: Routledge. **pp.9, 20, 45, 49, 55, 115, 121**

Jolley M (1989) The professionalisation of nursing: the uncertain path. In Jolley M, Allan P (Eds) Current Issues in Nursing. London: Chapman & Hall. pp. 1–22. **p.33**

Jones A (1996) Clinical supervision: a framework for practice. International Journal of Psychiatric Nursing Research 3 (1): 290–307. **p.100**

Jones H (1994) Health and Society in Twentieth-Century Britain. London: Longman. **p.22**

Jones K (1988) Experience in Mental Health: Community Care and Social Policy. London: Sage. **p.113**

Jones SG (Ed.) (1995) Cybersociety. London: Sage. **p.7**

Joseph M (1994) Sociology for Nursing and Health Care. Cambridge: Polity Press. **p.21**

Kalman N, Waughfield CG (1993) Mental Health Concepts. Nelson, USA: Delmar. **p.97**

Kaufman H (1981) The Administrative Behavior of Federal Chiefs. Washington DC: Brookings Institute.

Kane E (1984) Doing Your Own Research. London: Marion Boyers. **p.72**

Kane RA (1975) Interprofessional Teamwork. Manpower Monograph, 8. Syracuse, USA: Syracuse University School of Social Work. **p.54**

Keat R, Urry J (1975) Social Theory as Science. London: Routledge.

Kelly MP, Field D (1994) Comments on the rejection of the bio-medical model in sociological discourse. Medical Sociological News 19 (2): 34–7. **p.97**

Kidder LH (1981) (4th edn) Sellitz Wrightsman and Cook's Research Methods in Social Relations. New York: Holt, Rinehart and Winston. **p.72**

Kogan M, Redfern S, with Kober A, Norman IJ, Packwood T, Robinson S (1995) Making Use of Clinical Audit: A Guide to Practice in the Health Professions. Buckingham: Open University Press. **p.22**

Lankshear A, Brown J, Thompson C (1996) Mapping the nursing competencies required in institutional and community settings in preparation for parts 12 and 13 of the Register in the context of multidisciplinary health care provision (an exploratory study): ENB Research Highlight 16. London: ENB.

Larkin G (1983) Occupational Monopoly and Modern Medicine. London: Tavistock.

Larson MS (1977) The Rise of Professionalism. Berkeley: University of California Press. **pp.16,17**

Launer M (1996) Positive thoughts for negative minds. The Guardian, June 5. **p.5**

Layder D (1990) The Realist Image in Social Science. Cambridge: Polity.

Layder D (1993) New Strategies in Social Research. Cambridge: Polity.

Layder D (1994) Understanding Social Theory. London: Sage. **p.3**

LeCompte MD, Goetz JP (1982) Problems of reliability and validity in ethnographic research. Review of Educational Research 52 (1): 31–60. **p.73**

Leopoldt H (1979) Community psychiatric nursing. Nursing Times 75: 57–9. **p.52**

Lindesmith AR (1968) Addiction and Opiates. Chicago: Aldine.

Lyotard J (1985) The Postmodern Condition. Minneapolis: University of Minneapolis Press.

McAndrew PS (1996) A Survey to Determine Action That Has Been Undertaken In Relation To The Specific Recommendations Contained Within The Board's Response Paper To Working in Partnership: A Collaborative Approach To Care – Department of Health (1994). York: English National Board For Nursing, Midwifery and Health Visiting. **p.126**

McCulloch J (1995) Colonial Psychiatry and The African Mind. Cambridge: Cambridge University Press. **p.9**

McGuffin P, Murray R (Eds) (1991) The New Genetics of Mental Illness: London: The Mental Health Foundation.

McIntegart J (1990) A dying breed? Nursing Times 86 (39): 72. **p.118**

McKendrick D (1980) Statistical Returns: An Examination of Quantitative Methods in Use to Record the Activities of Community Psychiatric Nurses and Community Psychiatric Nursing Teams. Research Monograph, 43. Manchester: Manchester Polytechnic.

McKeown T (1979) (2nd edn) The Role of Medicine: Dream, Mirage or Nemesis. Oxford: Blackwell Scientific. **p.28**

McKinlay J, Stoeckle J (1988) Corporatization and the social transformation of doctoring. International Journal of Health Services 18 (2): 191–205. **pp.12, 20**

Maclean L (1995) Community Psychiatric Nurses in Relation to Diversion Schemes: In Brooker C, White E (Eds) Community Psychiatric Nursing: A Research Perspective Volume 3. London: Chapman & Hall. pp. 154–77. **p.121**

Macleod Clark J, Maben J, Jones K (1996) Project 2000: Perceptions of the Philosophy and Practice of Nursing. London: English National Board for Nursing, Midwifery and Health Visiting. **pp.35, 36**

McQuail D (1984) (2nd edn) Communication. Harlow: Longman.

McRobbie A, Thornton SL (1995) Rethinking moral panic for multi-mediated social worlds. British Journal of Sociology 46 (4): 559–74.

Malhotra VA (1987) Teaching of clinical sociology: Habermas' sociological theory as a basis for clinical practice with small groups. Clinical Sociology Review 5: 181–92.

Mangen SP, Griffith JH (1982) Community psychiatric services in Britain: the need for policy and planning. International Journal of Nursing Studies 19 (3): 157–66. **pp.48, 52**

Manis JG, Meltzer BN (Eds) (1967) Symbolic Interactionism: A Reader in Social Psychology. Boston: Allyn and Bacon.

Marx K (1969) Capital Vol. IV: Theories of Surplus Value. London: Burns. **p.118**

Masson J (1990) Against Therapy. London: Fontana.

Mathews R (1993) Squaring up to crime. Sociology Review, February: 26–29. **p.4**

May AR (1965) The psychiatric nurse in the community. Nursing Mirror, 31 December: 409–10. **p.48**

Means R, Smith R (1994) Community Care: Policy and Practice. Basingstoke: Macmillan. **p.113**

Melia K (1984) Student nurses: construction of occupational socialisation. Sociology of Health and Illness 6: 132–51.

Melia K (1987) Learning and Working: The Occupational Socialisation of Nurses. London: Tavistock. **p.39**

Mihill C (1992) Initiatives failing to save mentally ill from tragedy. The Guardian, 2 June.

Mihill C (1994) Problem doctors 'difficult to sack'. The Guardian, 13 May. **p.25**

Mihill C (1996) Doctors seek patient remedy. The Guardian, 14 June. **p.30**

Mihill C (1997a) Ten million lives will be saved in new TB strategy. The Guardian, 20 March. **p.29**

Mihill C (1997b) Midwife service 'too costly'. The Guardian, 14 February. **p.40**

Milburn A (1996) Labour's approach to mental health policy. Mental Health Nursing 16 (3): 8–10. **p.117**

Miller P, Rose N (Eds) (1986) The Power of Psychiatry. Cambridge: Polity Press. **pp.51, 113, 114**

Milne D (1988) Evaluating Mental Health Practice. Beckenham: Croom Helm.

Mollica RF (1980) Community mental health centres: an American response to Kathleen Jones. Journal of the Royal Society of Medicine 73, December: 836–68. **p.53**

Moore W (1997) High price of silence. The Guardian, 12 February. **p.22**

Morcom C, Hughes R (1996) How can clinical supervision become a real vision for the future? Journal of Psychiatric and Mental Health Nursing 3: 117–24. **p.100**

Morgan M, Calnan M, Manning N (1985) Sociological Approaches to Health and Medicine. London: Croom Helm. **pp.8, 15, 16**

Morrall PA (1987a) Recarceration. Unpublished MSc Dissertation. London: University of the South Bank. **p.111**

Morrall PA (1987b) Recarceration: social factors influencing admission to psychiatric institutions, and the role of the community psychiatric nurse as agent of social control: Community Psychiatric Nursing Journal 7 (6): 25–32. **p.111**

Morrall PA (1989a) The professionalisation of community psychiatric nursing: a review. Community Psychiatric Nursing Journal 9 (4): 14–22.

Morrall PA (1989b) Quality assurance in nurse education – the social context of learning. Nurse Education Today 9: 236–41. **p.41**

Morrall PA (1992) Transferable skills and community psychiatric nursing. Community Psychiatric Nursing Journal 5 (12): 14–18.

Morrall PA (1993) The beginning of the end of andragogy. Senior Nurse 13 (5): 42–4.

Morrall PA (1995a) The Professional Status of the Community Psychiatric Nurse. PhD Thesis. Loughborough: University of Loughborough. **pp.58, 72**

Morrall PA (1995b) Clinical autonomy and the community psychiatric nurse. Mental Health Nursing 15 (2): 16–19.

Morrall PA (1995c) Social Factors Affecting Communication. In: Ellis R B, Gates R J, Kenworthy N (Eds) Interpersonal Communication in Nursing. Edinburgh: Churchill Livingstone. **pp.21, 125**

Morrall PA (1996) Clinical sociology in the empowerment of clients. Mental Health Nursing 16 (3): 24–7. **pp.119, 126**

Morrall PA (1997) Lacking in rigour: a case-study of the professional practice of psychiatric nurses in four community mental health teams. Journal of Mental Health 6 (2): 173–9.

Morrow RA with Brown DD (1994) Critical Theory and Methodology. London: Sage.

Muir H (1993) Surgeons want nurses to help in operations. The Independent, 19 April. **p.37**

Munro BH, Page EB (1993) Statistical Methods for Health Care Research. Philadelphia: Lippincott.

Murphy E (1991) After the Asylums. London: Faber and Faber. **pp.11, 50, 115**

Murphy R (1990) Proletarianization and bureaucratization: the fall of the professional?. In Torstendahl R, Burrage M (Eds) The Formation of the Professions. London: Sage.

National Health Service Management Executive (1994) Introduction of Supervision Registers for Mentally Ill People from April 1994. London: HMSO. **pp.56, 118**

National Health Service Management Executive (1996) Primary Care: The Future. London: Department of Health. **p.18**

National Schizophrenic Fellowship (1992) Slipping Through the Net. Surbiton: NSF. **p.119**

Navarro V (1979) Medicine Under Capitalism. New York: Prodist. **p.11**

Nettleton S (1995) The Sociology of Health and Illness. London: Sage. **pp.9, 15, 20, 21 ,24**

Nightingale F (1859) Notes on Nursing. Glasgow: Blackie. **p.34**

Nolan P (1990) Psychiatric nursing – the first 100 years. Senior Nurse 10 (10): 20–3. **p.45**

Nolan P (1993) A History of Mental Health Nursing. London: Chapman & Hall. **pp.44, 45, 110**

Noon M (1988) Teams: the best option? The Health Service Journal, 6 October: 1160–1. **pp.54, 55**

Norusis MJ (1993) SPSS for Windows Basic System Users Guide Release 6.0. Chicago: SPSS.

Nuland SB (1996) An epidemic of discovery. Time (special issue) 148 (14): 8–13. **p.27**

Nye R (1996) The Citizen's Charter Five Years On (Memorandum). London: Social Market Foundation. **pp.29, 30**

Oakley A (1981) Interviewing women: a contradiction in terms. In Roberts H (Ed) Doing Feminist Research. London: Routledge and Kegan Paul.

O'Connor F (1994) The story of Clifford. The Guardian, 3 June. **p.119**

Onyett S, Heppleston T, Bushnell D (1994) A national survey of community mental health teams. Team Structures and process. Journal of Mental Health 3: 175–94. **p.104**

OPCS (1995) Surveys of Psychiatric Morbidity in Great Britain. Bulletin No.1, The prevalence of psychiatric morbidity among adults aged 16–64 living in private households in Great Britain. London: OPCS.

Oppenheim AN (1966) Questionnaire Design and Attitude Measurement. London: Heinemann.

Oppenheimer M (1973) The proletarianisation of the professional. Sociological Review Monograph 20: 213–37. **p.20**

Osgood CE , Suci GJ, Tannenbaum PH (1957) The Measurement of Meaning. Urbana: University of Illinois Press.

Øvretveit J (1993) Coordinating Community Care: Multidisciplinary Teams and Care Management. Buckingham: Open University Press. **pp.53, 55, 56, 101**

Owen J (1994) The view from within: cognitive behavioural assessment in schizophrenia. Psychiatric Care, March/April: 10–14. **p.118**

Owens P, Glennerster H (1990) Nurses in Conflict. London: Macmillan. **p.41**

Palmer A, Burns S, Bulman C (Eds) (1994) Reflective Practice in Nursing: The Growth of the Professional Practitioner. Oxford: Blackwell. **p.97**

Palmer VM (1928) Field Studies in Sociology: A Student's Manual. Chicago: University of Chicago Press.

Paquette M, Meal M, Rodemich C (1991) Psychiatric Nursing Diagnosis Care Plans For DSM–111–R. London: Jones & Bartlett. **p.97**

Parnell JW (1978) Community Psychiatric Nurses: An Abridged Version of the Report of a Descriptive Study. London: The Queens Nursing Institute. **pp.63, 64**

Parsons T (1949) Essays in Sociological Theory. Glencoe: Free Press. **p.8**

Parsons T (1951) The Social System. London: Routlege and Kegan Paul.

Parsons T (1954) Essays in Sociological Theory. New York: Free Press.

Patel K (1995) Shot in the arm for TB. The Times Higher Education Supplement, 26. **pp.28–29**

Patients Association (1994) Mental health nursing: a spectrum of skills. Mental Health Nursing 14 (3): 6–8.

Patmore D, Weaver T (1989) A measure of care. Health Service Journal, 99(5142), 330–1. **p.53**

Pawson R (1989) A Measure for Measures. London: Routledge.

Peay J (Ed) (1996) Inquiries After Homicide. London: Duckworth. **pp.112, 115**

Peplau HE (1994) Psychiatric mental health nursing: challenge and change. Journal of Psychiatric and Mental Health Nursing 1 (1): 3–7. **pp.1,43**

Petroyiannaki M, Raymond M (1978) How one community psychiatric nursing service works. Journal of Community Nursing. February, 21. **p.54**

Phillips BS (1966) Social Research: Strategy and Tactics. London: Collier-Macmillan.

Pilgrim D, Rogers A (1993) A Sociology of Mental Health and Illness. Buckingham: Open University Press. **pp.12, 47, 113**

Pilgrim D, Rogers A (1994) Something old, something new ... sociology and the organisation of psychiatry. Sociology 28 (2): 521–38.

Pollock LC (1986a) An evaluation research study of community psychiatric nursing employing the personal questionnaire rapid scaling technique. Community Psychiatric Nursing Journal, May/June: 11–21. **p.48**

Pollock LC (1986b) An introduction to the use of repertory grid technique as a research method and clinical tool for psychiatric nurses. Journal of Advanced Nursing 11: 439–45.

Pollock LC (1988) The work of community psychiatric nursing. Journal of Advanced Nursing 13: 537–45.

Pollock LC (1989) Community Psychiatric Nursing: Myth and Reality. London: Scutari. **pp.53–54, 115**

Pollock L (1990) The Goals and Objectives of community Psychiatric Nursing. In: Brooker C (Ed) Community Psychiatric Nursing: a Research Perspective. London: Chapman & Hall, pp. 113–43. **p.111**

Pope B (1985) Psychiatry in transition – implications for psychiatric nursing. Community Psychiatric Nursing Journal, July/August: 7–13.

Porter H (1994) Fears of tomorrow. The Guardian, 19 December. **p.26**

Porter R (1987) A Social History of Madness: Stories of the Insane. London: Weidenfeld & Nicolson. **pp.44–45, 125**

Porter R (1993) Everybody's talking about me. The Observer, 10 January. **p.119**

Porter R (1996) Trust me, I'm a doctor. The Observer Review, 16 June. **pp.16,25**

Porter S (1991) A participant observation study of power relations between nurses and doctors in a general hospital. Journal of Advanced Nursing 16: 728–35. **p.23**

Porter S (1996) Contra-Foucault: soldiers, nurses and power. Sociology 30 (1): 59–78. **p.41**

Power A (1992) The audit society. Unpublished paper presented to the History of the Present Study Group. London. **p.31**

Prins H (1995) (2nd edn) Offenders, Deviants or Patients? London: Routledge. **p.123**

Prior L (1993) The Social Organisation of Mental Illness. London: Sage. **p.46**

Rafferty AM (1996) The Politics of Nursing Knowledge. London: Routledge. **p.33**

Ramon S (1996) Mental Health in Europe: Ends, Beginnings and Rediscoveries. London: Macmillan/MIND. **pp.123, 124**

Rebach HM, Bruhn JG (1991) Handbook of Clinical Sociology. London: Plenum. **p.126**

Reed J, Proctor S (1993) Nurse Education: A Reflective Approach. London: Edward Arnold. **p.97**

Rees D (1995) Science for the good life. The Times Higher education Supplement, 11 August. **p.29**

Richman J (1987) Medicine and Health. London: Longman. **pp.10, 13**

Riska E, Weger K (Eds) (1993) Gender, Work and Medicine: Women and the Medical Division of Labour. London: Sage. **p.9**

Ritchie JH (1994) (Chairperson) The Report of the Inquiry into the Care and Treatment of Christopher Clunis. Presented to the Chairman of North East Thames and South East Thames Regional Health Authorities. London: HMSO. **pp.81, 112, 117, 119**

Robertson H, Scott DJ (1985) Community psychiatric nursing: a survey of patients and problems. Journal of the Royal College of General Practitioners 35: 130–2. **p.53**

Robinson WS (1951) The logical structure of analytical induction. American Sociological Review 16 (6): 812–18.

Rogers A, Pilgrim D (1996) Mental Health Policy in Britain. Basingstoke: Macmillan. **pp.18, 20, 46, 48, 53, 54, 113**

Rogers A, Pilgrim D, Lacey R (1993) Experiencing Psychiatry: User's Views of Services. Basingstoke: Macmillan/MIND.

Rogers B (1994) CPNs have kept pace with changing needs. Nursing Times 90 (25): 42.

Rogers CR (1961) On Becoming A Person: A Therapist's View of Psychotherapy. London: Constable.

Rogers SW (1991) Explaining Health and Illness: An Exploration of Diversity. Hemel Hempstead: Harvester Wheatsheaf. **p.2**

Rose A (Ed) (1962) Human Behaviour and Social Processes: an Interactionist Approach. London: Routledge and Kegan Paul.

Rose N (1986) Psychiatry: the discipline of mental health. In Miller P, Rose N (Eds) The Power of Psychiatry. Cambridge: Polity Press. **p.51**

Rosenhan DL (1973) On being sane in insane places. Science 179: 250–8.

Rosenthal M (1994) The Incompetent Doctor: Behind Closed Doors. Buckingham: Open University Press.

Rousseau J (1762, reprinted 1973) The Social Contract. London: Dent. **p.123**

Russell D (1995) Women, Madness and Medicine. Cambridge: Polity Press. **pp.9, 18**

Ryan T (1994) Perspectives and policy in mental illness. Senior Nurse 13 (7): 13–17.

Sainsbury Centre for Mental Health (1997) Pulling together. London: Sainsbury Centre. **pp.2, 43**

Saks M (1983) Removing the blinkers? A Critique of recent contributions to the sociology of professions. Sociological Review 31 (1): 1–21. **pp.7, 8**

Saks M (1995) Professions and Public Interest. London: Routledge. **pp.16, 21**

Salvage J (1985) The Politics of Nursing. London: Heinemann. **p.35**

Salvage J (1988) Professionalisation – or struggle for survival? A consideration of current proposals for the reform of nursing in the United Kingdom. Journal of Advanced Nursing 13: 515–19. **p.39**

Salvage J (1992) The new nursing: empowering patients or empowering nurses? In Robinson J, Gray A, Elkan R (Eds) Policy Issues in Nursing. Buckingham: Open University Press.

Samson C (1995) The fracturing of medical dominance in British Psychiatry. Sociology of Health and Illness, 17 (2): 245–69. **p.18**

Sapsford R, Abbott P (1992) Research Methods for Nurses and the Caring Professions. Buckingham: Open University.

Sayce L (1989) Community mental health centres – rhetoric or reality? In Brackx A, Grimshaw C (Eds) Mental Health Care in Crisis. London: Pluto. pp. 158–74. **p.53**

Sayce L, Graig T, Boardman A (1991) The development of community health centres in the UK. Social Psychiatry and Psychiatric Epidemiology 26: 14–20. **p.53**

Schwartz H, Jacobs J (1979) Qualitative Sociology: A Method to the Madness. New York: Free Press.

Scull AT (1979) Museums of Madness: The Social Organisation of Insanity in Nineteenth-Century England. Harmondsworth: Penguin. **pp.11, 12, 18, 44, 50**

Scull AT (1981) Social History of Psychiatry in the Victorial Era. In: Scull A T (Ed) Madhouses, Mad–doctors and Madmen. Philadelphia: University of Philadelphia Press. pp. 5–32. **p.44**

Scull AT (1983) The asylum as community or the community as asylum: paradoxes and contradictions of mental health care. In Bean P (Ed) Mental Illness: Changes and Trends. Chichester: John Wiley & Sons. pp. 329–50. **pp.11, 52, 114**

Scull AT (1984) (2nd edn) Decarceration: Community Treatment and the Deviant – a Radical View. Cambridge: Polity Press. **pp.11, 52, 114, 115**

Scull AT (1993) The Most Solitary of Afflictions: Madness and Society in Britain, 1700–1900. New Haven: Yale University Press. **pp.4, 18, 44, 46, 50**

Seedhouse D (1991) Liberating Medicine. Chichester: John Wiley & Sons. **p.27**

Severinsson EI (1995) Clinical Supervision in Health Care. Goteborg, Sweden: Nordic School of Public Health. **p.99**

Shapiro MB (1981) A method of measuring psychological changes specific to the individual psychiatric patient. British Journal of Medical Psychology 34: 151–5.

Sharpe D (1982) GP's views of community psychiatric nurses. Nursing Times, October 6-12, 78 (40): 1664–6. **p.111**

Sheppard M (1991) Mental Health Work in the Community. London: Falmer Press. **pp.50, 52, 116**

Sieber SD (1973) The integration of fieldwork and survey methods. In Burgess RG (Ed) (1982) Field Research: A Sourcebook and Field Manual. London: Allen and Unwin.

Simmons S (1988) Community psychiatric nurses and multidisciplinary working. Community Psychiatric Nursing Journal 8, September: 14–18. **pp.54, 55**

Simpson K (1986) Cumberledge and the CPN. Community Psychiatric Nursing Journal 6 (4) September/October: 6–10. **pp.53, 55**

Simpson K (1988) Medical power – the CPN's millstone? Community Psychiatric Nursing Journal 8 (3): 5–11. **pp.50, 111**

Simpson K (1989) Community psychiatric nursing – a research-based profession? Journal of Advanced Nursing 14 (7): 274–80.

Sims A (1993) quoted in Brindle D, Schizophrenia warning by psychiatrists' leader. The Guardian, 7 July. **p.119**

Skidmore D (1984) Muddling through. Nursing Times: Community Outlook, 9 May: 179–81.

Skidmore D (1986) The effectiveness of community psychiatric nursing teams and base locations. In Brooking J (Ed) Readings in Psychiatric Nursing Research. Chichester: Wiley. pp. 233–43.

Sladden S (1979) Psychiatric Nursing in the Community: A Study of a Working Situation. Edinburgh: Churchill Livingstone. **p.48**

Smail D (1984) Illusion and Reality: the Meaning of Anxiety. London: Dent.

Smith P (1993) Nursing as an occupation. In Taylor S, Field D (Eds) Sociology of Health and Health Care. Oxford: Blackwell. pp. 205–21. **pp.35, 36**

Social Services Committee (1985) Second Report. Community Care with Special Reference to Adult Mentally Ill and Mentally Handicapped People. London: HMSO. **p.53**

Spinelli E (1994) Demystifying Therapy. London: Constable. **p.118**

Spradley JP (1980) Participant Observation. New York: Holt, Rinehart and Winston.

Staff Reporters (1995) Police had a gutsful. The Evening Standard, Palmerston North, New Zealand, 26 October.

Stanley L (1990) Doing ethnography, writing ethnography: a comment on Hammersley. Sociology 24 (4): 617–27.

Stein LI (1967) The doctor-nurse game. Archives of General Psychiatry 16: 699–703. **pp.22, 105**

Strauss A (1978) Negotiations: Varieties, Contexts, Processes and Social Order. San Francisco: Jossey-Bass.

Strauss A, Schatzam L, Bucher R, Ehrlich D, Sabshin M (1964) Psychiatric Ideologies and Institutions. New York: Free Press.

Strauss A, Schatzam L, Ehrlich D, Bucher R, Sabshin M (1963) The Hospital and its Negotiated Order. In Freidson E (Ed) The Hospital in Modern Society. New York: Free Press. pp. 147–69. **p.19**

Sturt J, Waters H (1985) Role of the psychiatrists in community-based mental health care. Lancet, 8427 2 March: 507–8. **p.51**

Tattersall R (1992) Towards an Understanding of Power in the Medical Profession. Unpublished thesis. Sheffield: University of Sheffield. **p.23**

Taylor S, Field D (Eds) (1993) Sociology of Health and Health Care: An Introduction for Nurses. Oxford: Blackwell.

Tendler S (1995) Psychiatric nurse helps police to distinguish the mentally ill. The Times, 17 January. **p.121**

Tester K (1993) The Life and Times of Post-modernity. London: Routledge. **p.7**

Timmins N (1995) 'Fat cats' join the queue for treatment. The Independent, 16 June. **p.25**

Timmins N (1996) GP reforms to revive cottage hospital care. The Independent, 11 June. **p.18**

Tolkien JR (1994) The Lord of the Rings. London: BCA. **p.1**

Tolliday H (1978) Clinical autonomy. In Jaques E (Ed) Health Services: Their Nature and Organisation and Role of Patients, Doctors, Nurses and Complementary Professions. London: Heinemann. pp. 32–52. **p.17**

Turner BA (1981) Some practical aspects of qualitative data analysis. Quality and Quantity 15: 225–47.

Turner BS (1987) Medical Power and Social Knowledge. London: Sage. **p.34**

Turner BS (1995) (2nd edn) Medical Power and Social Knowledge. London: Sage. **p.7, 11**

Turner RH (1953) The quest for universals in sociological research, The American Sociological Review 18 (3): 33–5.

U205 Course Team (1985) Medical Knowledge: Doubt and Certainty. Buckingham: Open University Press.

Van Maanen J (1988) Tales of the Field: On Writing Ethnography. Chicago: University of Chicago Press.

Vasil A (1995) Shipley wants answers on birth in street. The Dominion, Auckland, New Zealand, 26 October. **p.114**

Wakeford J (1981) From methods to practice: a critical note on the teaching of research practice to undergraduates. Sociology 15 (4): 505–12.

Walby S, Mackay L, Greenwell J, Soothill K (1994) Medicine and Nursing: Professions in a Changing Health Service. London: Sage. **p.24**

Wallis MA (1987) Profession and professionalism and the emerging profession of occupational therapy. British Journal of Occupational Therapy, part 1: 50 (8), 259-62; part 2: 50 (9), 300–2. **p.33**

Ward L (1993) Race equality and employment in the National Health Service. In Ahmad W (Ed) Race and Heath in Contemporary Britain, Buckingham: Open University Press. pp. 167–82. **p.9**

Waters M (1994) Modern Sociological Theory. London: Sage.

Watson G (1994) Multi-disciplinary working and co-operation in community care. Mental Health Nursing 14 (2): 18–21. **p.56**

Weatherall D (1995) Science and the Quiet Art: Medical Research and Patient Art. Oxford: Oxford University Press. **p.28**

Webb EJ, Campbell DT, Schwartz RD (1966) Unobtrusive Measures: Non-reactive Research in the Social Sciences. Chicago: Rand McNally.

Weleminsky J (1989) Personal communication – available on request. **p.107**

White EG (1983) If It's Beyond Me … Community Psychiatric Nurses in Relation to General Practice. Unpublished MSc dissertation, Cranfield Institute.

White EG (1986) Factors which influence general practitioners to refer to community psychiatric nurses. In Brooking J (Ed) Readings in Psychiatric Nursing Research. Chichester: Wiley. pp. 215–32. **pp.51, 53, 55**

White EG (1987) Psychiatrist Influence on Community Psychiatric Services Planning and Development, and its Implications for Community Psychiatric Nurses. Unpublished MSc dissertation, University of Surrey. **p.54**

White EG (1990) Psychiatrists' influence on the development of community psychiatric nursing services. In Brooker C (Ed) Community Psychiatric Nursing: A Research Perspective. London: Chapman & Hall. pp. 197–224. **pp.49, 51, 55**

White EG (1993) Community psychiatric nursing 1980 to 1990: a review of organisation, education and practice. In Brooker C, White E G (Eds) Community Psychiatric Nursing: A Research Perspective Volume 2. London: Chapman & Hall. pp. 1–26. **pp.48, 51**

White EG, Brooker C (1990) The care programme approach. Nursing Times 87

(12): 66–67. **p.56**

Whyte WF (1982) Interviewing in field research. In Burgess R (Ed) Field Research: a Sourcebook and Field Manual. London: George Allen and Unwin.

Williams F (1989) Social Policy. Cambridge: Polity Press. **p.9**

Williams R (1981) Learning to do field research: intimacy and Inquiry in social life. Sociology 15 (4): 557–64.

Williamson F, Little M, Lindsay WR (1981) Two community psychiatric nursing services compared. Nursing Times 77 (27): 105–7. **p.48**

Willis E (1990) (revised edn) Medical Dominance. Sydney: Allen and Unwin. **pp.7, 8, 39**

Wing JK, Olsen R (Eds) (1979) Community Care for the Mentally Disabled. Oxford: Oxford University Press. **p.12**

Witz A (1990) Patriarchy and professions: the gendered politics of occupational closure. Sociology 24 (4): 675–90. **p.8**

Witz A (1992) Profession and Patriarchy. London: Routledge. **p.12**

Wooff K, Goldberg DP (1988) Further observations on the practice of community care in Salford: differences between community psychiatric nurses and mental health social workers. British Journal of Psychiatry 153: 30–7. **pp.53, 54, 111**

Wooff K, Goldberg DP, Fryers T (1988) The practice of community psychiatric nursing and mental health social work in Salford: some implications for community care. British Journal of Psychiatry 152: 783–92. **p.111**

Wright EO (1980) Class, occupation and organisation. International Yearbook of Organisational Studies. London: Routledge & Kegan Paul. **p.12**

Wright S (1985) Conflict or co-operation? – an overview. Nursing Practice 1 (1): 32–9. **pp.22, 105**

Yin RK (1984) Case Study Research: Design and Methods. London: Sage.

Young J, Mathews R (1992) Rethinking Criminology: The Realist Debate. London: Sage.

Zelditch M (1982) Some methodological problems of field studies. In Burgess RG (Ed) Field Research: A Sourcebook and Field Manual. London: Allen and Unwin.

Zimmerman DH, Wieder DL (1977) The Diary: Diary-Interview Method. Urban Life 5 (4) January: 479–98. **pp.63, 64**

Znaniecki F (1934) The Method of Sociology. New York: Farrar and Rinehart.

Index